EASTERN PHILOSOPHY

A HANDBOOK FOR BEGINNERS

CHARLES THEFAUT

Contact: charlesthefaut@outlook.com

First paperback edition February 2022.

Book cover & interior design by Aeysha Mahmood.

ISBN: 9798808997738

About the Author:

Charles holds a BA in Philosophy from King's College London, and an MSc in Psychology from the University of Surrey. He has written on a range of topics such as Buddhism, AI, and environmental issues in various publications. He is from London.

We are what we think.
All that we are arises with our thoughts.
With our thoughts we make the world.
(Dhammapada, 1)

TABLE OF CONTENTS

Introduction

WHAT IS PHILOSOPHY?

The word 'Philosophy' is rooted in the ancient Greek 'Philosophia', which translates roughly to: 'lover of knowledge'. In the Western world, philosophy is and has been a discipline which attempts to answer the fundamental 'What is?' questions. For example: What is reality? What is knowledge? What is time? What is right or wrong morally? What is a good life?

The Oxford dictionary defines philosophy as: 'The study of the fundamental nature of knowledge, reality, and existence…'. The word fundamental is important, as philosophy attempts to probe foundational concepts which hold up other disciplines such as reality, time, God, the soul or language.

For example, if a scientist asks: 'how do we create a light-weight metal alloy for a racing car?', then the engineer asks: 'what is the optimal and safest way to build a car?' … The philosopher may ask, 'what do we mean by the word car?'

When building a car, when does it become one? Is it when the wheel is fitted? Must there be an engine? The philosopher wants to probe the fundamental concept of 'car' and its use. Not to be difficult, but to better understand how we use language and how our fundamental concepts are built. Broadly speaking, a common question for early Western philosophers was something like: 'What is a 'good' life?' What does the concept of 'good' entail?

Within Western philosophy there are of course many schools and strands. Analytic philosophy is now a dominant style in modern universities, and is known for a focus on language, meaning and rigorous assessment of arguments. Whereas Continental philosophy refers to a group of thinkers from mainland Europe (mainly 19th-20th century) and their ideas about self, life, ethics and other topics (which were distinct from the mainly Anglo-American analytic tradition). These are just two examples of many schools and traditions in the West. But it's useful to highlight that both Eastern and Western philosophy are huge groups full of sets and subsets of ideas, styles and traditions. What does tie Western philosophy together is a recognition of being rooted in the ancient Greek schools.

East and West

As mentioned, the Western world usually looks to the ancient Greek tradition as the foundation of modern philosophy, academia, science, and more broadly society. In many respects this is fair. However, the philosophical schools of the 'East' in many cases pre date the West, and then existed alongside them for thousands of years. Whilst there are clear differences between Eastern and Western traditions, there are definite overlaps in themes and intentions which group all together as philosophy.

The Eastern schools have such vast differences between them that they can in no sense be thought of as one 'block'. Each system of thought has its own history and context from which it grew.

For the purpose of this book, the word Eastern is taken to mean the schools of India and China, which have had significant influence on surrounding countries. The term can be problematic as it groups together a vast area, with diverse groups of people and cultures. However in the context of philosophy it has generally been used to distinguish the Asian traditions from the European.

Of course philosophy in Asia is not limited to China and India. There are schools of vast influence from Japan to Iran, and that's without mentioning the rich and deep history of Middle-Eastern philosophy. For the sake of this book however, five schools have been chosen which for various reasons have had the most influence on the wider world and the history of philosophy in their respective areas.

In the Indian and Chinese traditions, philosophy was often (but not always) associated with groups or 'schools' rather than just individual thinkers. Each school can be understood as a systematic group of ideas which evolved together to form a coherent whole. It can be useful to think of a school of philosophy as a framework, or structure which has been contributed to by many different people.

The book is intended to be a concise introduction to the core themes of five of the most influential schools of the East. There is no attempt made here to give an exhaustive or even in depth perspective on each school, it is a 'taster' to gain context and understanding. However a reader should come away ready to gain further insight.

Philosophy is an academic pursuit, and is often framed in complex and difficult terminology. Whilst there is often a good reason for this, here space is given for the beginner to learn the fundamentals or for people to revisit the basics.

It is sometimes rather lazily mentioned that all schools of Eastern philosophy say 'basically the same thing' in different ways. Hopefully this book will demonstrate that this is far from true, and that debate exists between each of these schools on core issues such as God, reality, the soul, salvation and politics.

Whilst there are great cultural and academic differences between the Indian and Chinese schools, one thing all the schools chosen to be described here have in common is a practical application to the improvement of life. As such, any reader of this book will be able to decide for themselves if they wish to apply any aspects to their own life, or consider how the issues discussed have shaped the society they live in today.

Whilst some reference is given to the chronology of the schools, (so as to better appreciate their context in history) this is not a history book or a study of sociology or society. The focus here is on distilling the core ideas.

Each school described here is closely interwoven with religion, culture and society. The Indian schools in particular are philosophical strands of religious movements and so should be treated as such. However care is taken here to stick to the philosophy, which is to say the systematic ideas and structure of each school, rather than to focus on the mystical or religious aspects.

The Indian philosophical tradition is often used to argue for or against various positions in orthodox Hinduism. Indian philosophy is rooted in the *Vedas,* ancient texts written in Sanskrit which form the basis of Indian civilisation and society. The history of Indian philosophy dates back to at least the *Upanishads* (one book of the *Vedas*). The *Upanishads* are thought to have been written around 700 BC. The *Vedas* themselves date to anywhere between 1500-1200 BC and may well have been orally transmitted before that.

The Chinese schools grew from an entirely unique context and culture. They tend to focus on social and political themes, as well as our relation to nature and the universe. They are often interwoven with Chinese traditional medicine, astrology and politics. There is a distinct character to the Chinese schools which defines them entirely apart from the Indian tradition and reflects the complex society from which they developed.

As with anything else, systems of ideas develop and change over time and with for example Buddhism, there are many schools which diverged in their focus and interpretation of the core texts. Here, as much as possible, the fundamental positions of each school has been described. Furthermore, there is a weight toward consensus and generally accepted interpretations of various issues. This is so as to give the reader the most broad and fundamental impression of each school.

It is not the aim of this book to cover new ground, or to suggest to the reader how they synthesise any issue into their own life or the modern world. Nor is it to proselytise any particular philosophy to the West. It is simply a guidebook for any traveller who wants firm grounding.

This book is written on the shoulders of, and in debt to many scholars and writers who have introduced these topics to the West. These are listed in the bibliography, but special mention should go to *A Sourcebook in Indian Philosophy* by Sarvepalli Radhakrishnan and Charles A. Moore, which despite being over fifty years old, still serves as an authoritative and comprehensive introduction to the Indian schools, and a source of some primary texts and concepts which have been used here.

There are of course many more than five major schools of Eastern philosophy, and any attempt to give the reader a full introduction to every school in one book would be difficult. Each school described here has been chosen due to one main factor; their influence.

It is likely that most of these schools will already be familiar to the reader by name and perhaps many of their core ideas will be too. The reader is asked to approach this book anew, with the spirit of 'back to basics'.

Whether it be via salvation of the mind, the betterment of society, or by reflecting nature- improving the human condition is the thread which binds these diverse schools together.

No idea is beyond criticism and nobody owns the truth. That is the spirit of philosophy.

Key terms

First, familiarise yourself with some key terms that will be used throughout this book, and some example questions in each category to give some context.

Epistemology: The study of what is and is not true knowledge.

For example: *'Can testimony or memory be considered as knowledge when both are error prone?'*

Ontology : The study of what is and isn't real in existence.

For example: *'What substances make up the universe? Is reality a simulation?'*

Logic: In the most basic form, it is the use of a premise and a subject to reach a conclusion.

For example: *'If all tables are wooden, then this particular table must be wooden'.*

Ethics: The enquiry into what is morally 'right' or 'wrong'.

For example: *'Does right or wrong exist? Is an action evil if it has a good intention but a bad outcome?'*

Direct Realism: The idea that objects external to us actually exist independently of us.

For example: *'If I see a tree, it exists independently of me'*

Idealism: The view that objects do not exist independently of perception and rely in some way on consciousness to exist.

For example: *'The tree I see, depends on my 'seeing' it, to exist'*

Dualism: The view that two substances exist, one material, and one non- material.

For example *'There is an immaterial soul and a physical body'*

Metaphysics: The enquiry into the nature of reality, comprising a broad range of issues such as- the soul, time, God, consciousness etc.

For example: *'Does God exist? Is Time linear or circular? Is reincarnation possible without a soul?'*

Chapter 1:

INTRODUCTION TO INDIAN PHILOSOPHY

India is a vast subcontinent, home to a multitude of languages, cultures and religions. The genesis of civilisation in India is generally traced to a bronze age culture known as 'Indus Valley', of which little is known. After the decline of that civilisation the next which is generally agreed to have emerged is the Vedic culture, which is defined by a group of texts called the *Vedas.*

India has an ancient philosophical tradition that dates at least back to the *Vedas*. Indian philosophy precedes the European tradition by hundreds of years, and to this day inspires great debate and reflection on the nature of life and the human condition.

The *Vedas* are a group of spiritual and philosophical texts written in Sanskrit, from which form the foundations of the Hindu religion. Sanskrit is an ancient south-Asian language that is traditionally associated with Vedic and Hindu culture.

The Vedas are thought to have been written roughly between 1700–1100 BC (although may have been transmitted orally before this, and many scholars date them earlier). They are a mix of history, myth, poetry, veneration and philosophy. They are widely thought to be the oldest existing texts written in an Indo-European language.

The *Vedas* were developed over hundreds (if not thousands) of years and are divided into four or five distinct categories. The most recent of these is the *Upanishads,* which address philosophy, ontology and meditation. It is the Upanishads which centrally defined the core of Hindu culture and religion for the millennia to follow. Later, Indian philosophy would split into schools that went on to produce *Sutras*, which are books of philosophy and spirituality developing further commentary on the *Vedas.*

Much of the *Upanishads* are devoted to developing the idea of the self or soul (Atman) and the ultimate reality or God (Brahman) and what their relationship is. Other topics include the illusory nature of our reality, meditation and critique of previously held rituals (such as sacrifice). There is also development of the idea of rebirth and description of techniques to obtain liberation and salvation. Each of these themes is developed and continued by the later schools.

Renowned scholar Sarvepalli Radhakrishnan grouped Indian philosophy into a timeline with four broad periods. Whilst there is no definitive cut off point between each period, his model (paraphrased and summarised below) serves to give an overview of the development of philosophy:

1. **The Vedic Period** (2500 BC- 600 BC). This period was defined by the development of the Vedas. One of

the later developed texts in this period was the *Upanishads,* which of all Vedic texts focused most on philosophical issues such as the nature of reality, liberation and suffering.

2. **The Epic Period** (600 BC – 200 AD) This period was defined by the development of the various orthodox and heterodox schools and their defining ideas and debates. Still largely oral, much of the material from this time will have been lost. The hugely important *Bhavagad Gita* was written at this time.

3. **The Sutra Period** (200 AD- roughly 1100 AD) The period when doctrines and treaties of various schools were further refined, then written down and codified into *Sutras,* which came to define and become the source texts for modern day study.

4. **The Scholastic Period** (roughly 1100 AD to 1600 BC) The period in which commentary, and secondary source texts became common, and fierce debate raged between schools based on commentary of the *Sutras.*

The Scholastic Period is generally considered to have ended when India's culture began to be influenced by outside forces such as Islamic and European Invasions. Indian philosophy did not 'stop' in the 17th century and has developed and continues to this day, however these generally defined periods help group the development into a structure.

Traditionally Indian philosophy is broken down into 'schools' rather than individuals. These schools would debate each other vigorously and sometimes group together and merge parts of their frameworks. Individuals would of course be prominent within the schools, and often revered for their contributions.

The Indian schools are often categorised as: orthodox or heterodox. The orthodox schools are those who accept the authority of the Upanishads. These are generally the Hindu schools. The heterodox schools are those which reject the ultimate authority of the Upanishads (however are often still influenced by them) These include the Buddhists and the Jains.

All the orthodox schools generally accept that existence entails suffering and that the soul (Atman) is trapped in this realm of existence (Samsara) due to action and reactions (Karma). Whilst devotion and worship are a focus, there is an equal focus on 'self work', and introspection, so the responsibility is on the individual to achieve liberation (Moksha) from this realm of existence.

Whilst there is great diversity of opinion between the major schools, there does exist common themes which, taken together, define a certain attitude to the world which characterises Indian philosophy.

Sarvepalli Radhakrishnan described these (paraphrased below):

- An intense focus on the spiritual part of life, and the belief that salvation in some sense is possible.
- The belief that there is something unsatisfactory in this life, which is caused in some sense by attachment or desire.
- The practical motivation that philosophy should be applicable in life (for salvation) and not just merely an intellectual pursuit.

- An introspective approach is necessary for discovering and discussing reality.
- Lived experience and intuition trump pure reason- there is space for direct knowledge via intuition that can then be explained by reason but not reached by it.
- Reverence and acceptance of the core authority of each school and continuation of their ideas.

Most (but not all) Indian schools considered existence to consist largely of suffering and argue that there are higher realms of existence with less suffering, and beyond that an ultimate 'liberation' - Moksha.

A key debate between schools was regarding how to achieve this liberation. This is what is known as their *soteriological* goal. From those debates each school developed detailed systems of ontology, epistemology, metaphysics and logic, known as their Darsana.

In this book we will focus on two orthodox Schools, the Yoga School and The Nyaya School. The Yoga school is grouped with and shares much of its framework with the Samkhya school. Likewise the Nyaya school shares much of its framework with the Vaisheshika school. We will also examine the Buddhist's, the best known heterodox school.

Before we delve into each school further, it is best to consider some key terminology which each relies upon (and in some cases rejects).

Atman: The non physical, eternal substrate which carries between lifetimes, and is bound to Samsara by Karma. In other words, the soul.

Samsara: The mundane reality we experience day to day. This is the realm of existence and rebirth, which the Atman repeatedly is born into. Often thought of as illusionary and unsatisfactory.

Karma: Translates roughly to action. In a broad sense, Karma is the idea that all actions create a reaction and are the result of a previous action. The concept is closely tied with ethics, and the idea of reincarnation. It is usually held that the 'fruit' of an action may bear in another lifetime, and is not necessarily immediate. Karma is often understood to be the force which continues the cycle of rebirth, by binding people to the material world.

Moksha: The ultimate liberation- the release of the Atman from Samsara.

Nitya: The concept of an absolute, unchanging existence.

Jiva: A living thing within Samsara, a combination of an Atman and the physical body in any given animal or human.

Brahman: Understood as a divine, omnipresent, formless cause of all that exists, and the underlying unifying principle behind everything. Brahman is constant, unchanging, above Karma, the first cause and the finality of all things. In other words, God.

Manas: Mental faculties or more broadly speaking, the mind.

Chapter 2:

YOGA

Yoga Is The Suppression Of The Modifications Of The Mind. (Yoga Sutra, 1.2)

Yoga is one of the six main schools of Hindu philosophy. It has had a remarkable influence on the world, with a resurgence in interest throughout the twentieth century. The school is notable particularly for its emphasis on practical steps (such as physical postures, meditation and controlled breathing) toward reaching a state of spiritual freedom called Moksha.

The Yoga and Samkhya schools accept the concepts of Karma, Moksha, Atman, Jiva and Brahman, discussed in the introduction. Yoga borrows much of its ontological framework from the Samkhya school, and applies this along with a human focused, practice based discipline aimed at liberation of the soul.

Patañjali (2nd-4th century BC), was an ancient Indian philosopher, sage and polymath, who is regarded as the founder of the Yoga system. He is generally regarded as the author of the primary texts, (*Yoga Sutras*) which were written in Sanskrit. He is considered a sage and figure of worship by many Hindus. Patañjali is also thought to have authored a number of other important historical texts, such as medical and grammatical works (there is debate around authorship of some of these).

The *Yoga Sutras are* generally understood to be a commentary upon, and synthesis of many older works and traditions, most of which are now lost to history. There is debate as to how much of this text is the original work of Patañjali, and how much is commentary upon older texts. Either way, he is generally regarded as the one who compiled, edited and refined them.

The *Yoga Sutras* read like an intricate instruction manual towards spiritual liberation, with great care taken to describe each element of the system such as meditation, postures, breath-control, chanting and concentration. They are a combination of psychology, spirituality, and the study of consciousness. They are religious texts as much as they are philosophical, with regular reference to the soul and God.

It is likely that many of the physical postures and meditative practises included in Yoga predate Hinduism, and have existed on the Indian subcontinent for well over three thousand years, continually evolving. They are likely originally based on observation of animals and nature, and are a shared heritage of hundreds of cultures from the region.

In this chapter, we will refer to Yoga as the philosophy expounded in the *Yoga Sutras,* rather than any modern conception of it as purely an exercise.

Many commentaries describe Samkhya-Yoga as one system taken together. Samkhya can be thought of as the metaphysical, epistemological framework, developed from the Vedas. Whilst the attitude of Yoga is to accept these principles, with an added disciplined practice.

The philosophy of Samkhya, may be thought of as the fundamental Hindu position, which takes this basic form:

- Reality (Samsara) is composed of two fundamental substances: Prakriti (material nature) and Purusa (the non-material, consciousness).
- These substances are eternal, and un-caused.

- Souls (Atman), are eternally reborn into Samsara, as a result of the bonds of action and reaction (Karma).
- Souls can be liberated from this bond, and achieve eternal freedom (Moksha).
- Liberation is acheived by separating their non material consciousness from the material realm. This is achieved via correct knowledge, and practises.

Yoga then accepts this Samkhya basis and goes on to develop a detailed set of practises for the practical goal of achieving liberation.

What is Yoga?

Yoga is a system of ideas and practises, designed to attain a heightened state of awareness and human potential, via a system of behaviours, abstentions, physical postures and exercises. Someone who practises Yoga may be called a yogi.

The ultimate goal of Yoga can be described in many ways, one word is 'freedom'. Freedom from the entrapment of consciousness in the material realm. To free the soul from the endless cycle of death and rebirth which it is subject to. Yoga is fundamentally a practical, applicable system for the adherent to follow.

The first step toward attaining freedom in Yoga, is to withdraw and abstain from actions and behaviours that cloud our true sense of things, such as lust, desire, lying and greed. One must first 'clear the waters' before one can move toward further action. The next step is to engage in the practises which are conducive to Moksha, such as postures, chanting, meditation, and breath control.

Whilst there is a complex and vast underlying system of thought from which it developed, the focus of Yoga is not intellectual. The focus is the practical steps. The *Yoga Sutras* are written like an instruction manual focused on imparting the fine details of each of the exercises, practises and abstentions.

Yoga is contemplation. The word "Yoga" is derived from the root yuj, to contemplate. (Yoga Sutra, 1.1 (commentary by Vsaya))

Dualism

Yoga is a dualistic school. Building from the Samkhya tradition, it argues that two fundamental 'substances' or 'forces' exist, the combination of which creates reality. These substances are called Prakriti and Purusa.

Prakriti is a word that represents all material things in the universe, a rough translation might be 'nature'. That would include all observable objects and their individual parts e.g. a table, wood, a bottle, a car... Prakriti is understood to be impermanent, ever changing, and subject to the laws of cause and effect.

Purusa is a word that represents consciousness and the immaterial elements of reality, and may be roughly translated as 'spirit'. Purusa is understood to be permanent, unchanging, and also to be un-caused.

Human beings (and all living things) are understood to be a combination of Purusa (the soul, consciousness) and Prakriti (the body, mind). Living things which combine nature and spirit in this way are known as *Jiva.*

In the Yoga system (unlike in Western dualism) the mind is designated as being material (Prakriti). The mind being understood as thoughts and rational processes. It is the consciousness, higher self, or 'soul' which is understood to be the 'Purusa' aspect of human existence (more on this distinction later).

Therefore in Yoga, it is thought that one has a limited and unfulfilled understanding of life if they think the material aspect of life is all there is. One must recognise that their consciousness is immaterial and eternal, in order to have a complete understanding of reality.

A goal of Yoga, is to 'separate' the Purusa from the Prakriti within oneself (as they have become 'bound'), in order to attain Moksha and escape the day to day mental states which keep us trapped.

When there is equal purity between the intelligence energy of material nature and the spirit, then there is total separation from the mundane psychology.
(Yoga Sutra, 3.55)

The Eight Limbs of Yoga

Patañjali wrote that there are eight components (or 'limbs') of yogic practice, which should be used together to obtain freedom from ignorance and the bonds to the material world.

These eight limbs start with external behaviours and then progress toward an inward focus on self. They are to be practised in order, leading to the final step- Samadhi, which precedes Moksha (see below). They are as follows:

1. Abstinences

Abstinences or *Yama* are described as moral duties which one should practice in order to progress on the path to freedom, and defined as negative actions to abstain from. They are listed as:

Violence (or injuring another), lying, stealing, infidelity and greed.

2. Observances

The observances or *Niyamas* are a positive set of practises one should engage in, in order to progress further on the path to freedom. These are:

Contentment, cleanliness (of mind and body), study (of self and the yogic texts), discipline and surrender to God or a higher force.

3. Breath-control

Breath-control or *Pranayama* is the practice of consciously regulating breath, in order to reach a desired mental state of calm and focus, as well as expelling toxins. The *Yoga Sutra* describes techniques for breath-control in intricate detail which are to be followed carefully by the adherent.

4. **Physical postures**

Postures are physical aids to concentration (these are what people often think of when the word Yoga comes to mind). Mastering of the correct physical postures is said to ease disturbances. The postures are inspired by ancient pre Vedic Indian traditions, and detailed as an aid to a serene state of mind, rather than solely for the purpose of their physical benefits (although there are many).

5. **Withdrawal of the senses**

This is the process of removing external distracting stimuli, which keeps one in a state of desire and attachment to the material world (Prakriti). It is common for yogis to withdraw from society in isolation for prolonged periods of time to achieve this aim. Breath control is described as the technique needed to withdraw the senses.

The last three limbs are mental disciplines, to be taken together, in progression:

6. **Concentration**

Concentration or *Dharana* is understood as the 'steadfastness of the mind', a balanced mental state which is not wavered by extreme emotions or desires. It is a grounded and assured state.

7. Meditation

Meditation or *Dhyana* is a follow-on from concentration and understood as a subtle, non-intellectual reflection on the object of concentration. A 'flow of awareness'.

8. Absorption or oneness

Following on from concentration, and meditation, is absorption or *samadhi,* this is understood as becoming one with the subject of meditation, to engage with it without any further reflection or flow of thoughts. This is described as the ultimate state of awareness.

Samadhi then, is regarded as the highest form of consciousness available on the human plane, and a precursor to achieving Moksha. Samadhi is generally regarded as a mental state which can be reached after renunciation of attachment to any object in the material world. A common tactic for a Yoga teacher is to concentrate slowly on one external object to achieve *Dharana*, and then progress from there.

It may take many years of dedicated practice to achieve samadhi, and it is dependent on disciplined practice of the previous limbs of Yoga. Great will power (but not material desire) is needed to achieve samadhi.

Whilst there is recognition that one could achieve blissful or calm mental states spontaneously, or by other means (for example by socialising or by exercising) these are not considered to be yogic practice. Yoga is a discipline which is voluntarily focused along the specific path set out by the *Yoga Sutras*, as opposed to involuntary mental states which may be similar in nature, but do not serve the specific purpose of yogic practice.

Yama (Restraint), Niyama (Observance), Asana (Posture), Pranayama (Regulation Of Breath), Pratyahara (Withholding of Senses), Dharana (Fixity), Dhyana (Meditation) And Samadhi (Perfect Concentration) Are The Eight Means Of Attaining Yoga.
(Yoga Sutra, 2.29)

The Five Afflictions (Klesas)

Avidya (Misapprehension About The Real Nature Of Things), Asmita (Egoism), Raga (Attachment), Dvesa (Aversion) And Abhinivesa (Fear Of Death) Are The Five Klesas (Afflictions).
(Yoga Sutra, 2.4)

In addition to the eight limbs, the *Yoga Sutras* reference five 'afflictions' which are described as undesirable mental states which cause suffering and hinder the practice of Yoga. Anyone can be prone to these afflictions, so even experienced yogis will be wary of succumbing to them.

1. **Ignorance** (Avidya) is understood as one being unaware of the true nature of the universe (this will include the core concepts discussed above such as Karma, rebirth, Moksha etc.) This is importantly listed as the first affliction. Yoga philosophy recognises that whilst practical application is needed to achieve liberation, one must first have the correct knowledge to do so, and to know why one is doing so.

If one is in a state of ignorance, then they have no motivation to practice Yoga. Ignorance is viewed as the root affliction, which serves as a route to all others- it is most important to tackle this first for any yogi. Examples of ignorance may include:

- Misidentifying impermanent things as permanent
- Identifying only with the material world
- Believing that actions do not have reactions
- Believing there is no soul

Avidya Is The Breeding Ground For The Others [Klepas] Whether They Be Dormant, Attenuated, Interrupted Or Active. (Yoga Sutra, 2.4)

2. **Egoism** (Asmita). This is understood as a misidentification with the ego as being the true self, and therefore tending toward selfish action. Egoism leads to a false separation of reality and self and further rebirths. It can also mean misidentifying the true self (Purusa) with the instrument of knowledge or cognitive thought which is also known as Buddhi. In another sense, it may mean to identify the self as purely material.

Asmita Is Tantamount To The Identification Of Purusa Or Pure Consciousness With Buddhi. (Yoga Sutra, 2.6)

3. **Attachment** (Raga). Non attachment is a cornerstone of all the orthodox Hindu schools. Attachment is related to desire, which keeps one bound to the material world and unfocused on yogic practice. It can lead to many other negative mental states as a result of gain

or loss of the objects of attachment. In their most extreme forms attachments are like addictions, and are often associated with a temporary pleasure.

Attachment Is that (Modification) Which Follows Remembrance Of Pleasure.
(Yoga Sutra, 2.7)

4. **Aversion** (Dvesa). Aversion is described as an impulsive, negative mental state which is a result of external influence. It can be understood as a pattern based on previous experience. For example feeling disgust towards a wound, or anger towards a group of people who have hurt you before. Whilst these can be basic human emotions, a yogi avoids these, as a mind prone to aversion is controlled by outside forces and psychological impulses they cannot control. A yogi is encouraged to see the external world as neutral and avoid judgements.

Aversion Is That (Modification) Which Results From Misery.
(Yoga Sutra, 2.8)

5. **Fear of Death** (Abhinivesa). A condition recognised in all living things- this affliction is a form of ignorance from the yogic perspective, as it fails to recognise the nature of reality (as one fearing death will misidentify the physical body as the true self). Furthermore, fear itself is a state of suffering, which is a distraction from the path of Yoga and leads to misidentification with the material world.

As In The Ignorant So In The Learned
The Firmly Established Inborn Fear Of Annihilation
Is The Affliction Called Abhinivesa.
(Yoga Sutra, 2.9)

Patañjali argued that actions performed whilst in the mental state of these afflictions, will lead to impressions which will manifest in future life cycles, and keep one bound to the material plane.

The *Yoga Sutras* are clear in that to overcome these mental afflictions, one must first gain correct knowledge, and this knowledge can only be obtained via the practice of the eight limbs of Yoga, and study of the *Sutras*.

Mind and Consciousness distinction

As discussed, the dualism of Yoga divides consciousness (Purusa) and matter (Prakriti).

The mind is designated as being material (Prakriti), therefore consciousness, (which is Purusa) is distinguished from mind. As such, the Yoga school does not believe that the mind generates consciousness. They instead believe that consciousness experiences the mind.

But what do we exactly mean by mind and consciousness?

In the Yoga-Samkhya system, the mind is broken down into components, which are all designated as Prakriti. The main ones are listed below.

- *Manas-* Is described as the 'organ', 'perception', and 'categorisation' part of the mind, which takes in data from the outside world, and categorises it, and then makes decisions or analysis based on this data. This aspect of mind is shared with animals.

- *Buddhi*- Is understood to be a higher form of reason, or intellect, which the mind engages in when reflecting on data absorbed by the *Manas*. This is understood to be a highly complex, subtle form of Prakriti.

- *Ahankara*- The above two components of mind are 'impersonal' but the *Ahankara* is the 'ego' or 'self' aspect of mind, which allows mind to understand itself as separate from what it is perceiving, and to be its own entity.

So perception, thought, analysis, and ego or self are all designated as being material, and part of Prakriti. So what then is consciousness?

Consciousness is understood to be the unchanging, immaterial, formless awareness that underlies the material aspects of a living experience. It can navigate between different lifetimes or forms. This may be loosely compared to the Western concept of a 'soul'.

The Yoga school believes that the material aspects of the mind are 'illuminated' by the immaterial 'light' of consciousness.

So, the mental structures of mind are material, however an immaterial consciousness provides illumination, and acts as a silent 'witness' to this process, the two combining to form the human experience.

The immaterial (Purusa*)* element of life, is understood as bound, or tied, to the material (Prakriti) element, through many lifetimes. The ultimate goal of Yoga is the un-pairing of these two, the freeing of the 'soul' from material bonds.

This Yoga Sutra ties all of this together:

> ***...Liberation Is Realised When The Gunas (Having Provided For The Experience And Liberation Of Purusa) Are Without Any Objective To Fulfil And Disappear Into Their Causal Substance. In Other Words,***
> ***It Is Absolute Consciousness Established In Its Own Self.***
> ***(Yoga Sutra, 4.34)***

The Three Gunas

Prakriti (representing all material things), is broken down into three further elements, known as 'Gunas'. Each Guna is representative of a different property, type, or function of matter.

As mentioned, mind is considered an aspect of Prakriti, so the Gunas are applicable to mind as they are to unconscious matter. The three Gunas each have various Western translations which cover a broad area, these are:

1. **Sattva:** (harmony, balance, wholeness, oneness, non-violence, ethical virtue).
2. **Rajas:** (movement, action, passion, drive, ego).
3. **Tamas:** (imbalance, destruction, chaos, war, delusion, ignorance, dullness).

The Five Planes of the Mind

The planes of the mind are: Wandering (ksipta); forgetful (mudha); occasionally steady or distracted (viksipta); one-pointed (ekagra); and restrained (niruddha). (Yoga Sutra, 1.1 (commentary by Vsaya))

A popular commentary of the *Yoga Sutras* by the ancient Vedic sage Vsaya describes there being five 'planes' of the mind. These can be thought of as 'levels' or states of mind, starting with the most ignorant, and climbing toward the most conscious.

As mind is defined as material, these states all have the quality of Prakriti, and share in different aspects of the Gunas. The given planes of mind are:

1. **Wandering**: a restless state, defined by flitting between fixation on sensory objects, and is constantly moving and agitated.
2. **Forgetful**: here the mind is calmer, but is asleep, and tends to not absorb information, and is lazy.
3. **Distracted**: here the mind is more rational, and reflects on external stimuli, but lacks proper understanding and is easily distracted.
4. **Concentrated**: here the mind is largely in a state of 'sattva', highly concentrated.
5. **Restricted**: the mental modifications and ignorance are gone, impressions only remain.

Of these planes of mind, 'concentrated' and 'restricted' are considered to be conducive towards practising Yoga, and thus obtaining the ultimate freedom. The first three can be thought of as common states of mind which one has to work through and transcend.

Epistemology:

The Yoga school accepts three sources of valid knowledge: perception, inference and testimony.

Perception: This is split into internal and external perception. External perception is understood as perception taken directly from our senses or the material world. Internal perception is understood as a psychological function, in response to external stimuli.

Inference: Inference is understood as new knowledge gained by combining the results of one or more pieces of knowledge gained through perception. For example, inferring that a dog has been in your garden by examining footprints. Or inferring that water once existed in an area due to rock erosion. Inference is defined generally as a conclusion reached on the basis of evidence and reasoning.

Testimony: Testimony is understood to be a form of knowledge gained from the word of a trusted witness, or authority. Some Hindu schools reject this form of knowledge as it can of course be unreliable. However, the Yoga school allows it as long as the reliability of the testimony can be verified. They argued that testimonial knowledge is necessary to gain a proper understanding of the world, otherwise we would only have knowledge of our own limited experience. This is important to the Yoga school, as it relies on lineages of teachers to relay practical knowledge to students via testimony. The *Yoga Sutra* is in part testimonial.

Om

> ***The sacred word designating him is Pranava or the Mystic Syllable OM...repeat it and contemplate upon its meaning...from that comes realisation of the individual self And the obstacles are resolved...***
> ***(Yoga Sutra, 1.27-9)***

Om, (or *Aum*) throughout many Indian and Hindu texts is understood in various ways to be a primordial sound, force, and concept that pre-dates and sustains the universe. In this sense, it represents, or symbolises the concept of God as a creator, or at least an aspect of God. Om is designated as non material (Purusa).

One of the given practises of Yoga is to contemplate Om. This can be through chanting, or visualising the symbol of Om. The Om symbol is commonly taken to represent Yoga. However Om is not unique to the Yoga school and is a shared symbol and object of veneration throughout the Hindu religion.

The Yoga system regards the body as being to an extent 'impure' or 'unclean' as a result of its being of the material world. Therefore it is in need of cleansing through the correct practises such as breath work and postures.

Postures

Motionless And Agreeable Form (Of Staying) Is Asana (Yogic Posture).
(Yoga Sutra, 2.46)

The physical practice of postures is what most people in the West now associate with the word Yoga. Postures are reflective of the eight limbs of Yoga, viewed as an essential tool in obtaining absolute freedom.

The art of postures for exercise, physical health and spiritual purposes certainly predates the *Yoga Sutra* and there is evidence for the practice going back thousands of years before that on the Indian subcontinent.

The *Yoga Sutra* makes it clear that the purpose of physical postures is to aid concentration, and to overcome the competing physical stimuli (which are referred to as 'pairs of opposites') from the material world. This practice aids in liberating one's consciousness (Purusa) from their physical thoughts, and conditions (Prakriti).

When posture has been mastered he is not disturbed by the pairs of opposites such as heat and cold.
(Yoga Sutra, 1.48 (commentary by Vsaya))

The postures are not meant to be akin to strenuous exercise, and whilst they carry many physical benefits such as increased flexibility, strength and composure, their purpose is to garner the higher mental states which help one achieve Moksha.

The posture should be steady and comfortable... it results in relaxation of effort and meeting with the infinite. (Yoga sutra, 2.47)

A common starting point for the yogic postures is the 'lotus' posture, which involves sitting cross legged, back straight, and fingers clasped together; this is also often used to aid meditation.

Breath-control

The control of breath...the lengthening of the duration of the stay of the air outside the lungs. Let mental steadiness be optionally cultivated by these (Yoga sutra, 1.34 (Commentary by Vsaya))

The practice of breath control *(Pranayama)* is also an aid to concentration and absolute freedom. Yogis use breath control as a means of focus and to steady the mind to be free from distraction. *Vsaya* gave some specific instructions about how proper breath control is used to free oneself from the chain of 'cause and effect' and rebirth.

'This karma of the yogi which covers up the light and binds him to repeated births, becomes weak by the practice of control of breath every moment, and is then destroyed...' (Yoga Sutra, 2.52 (commentary by Vsaya))

There are complex descriptions of various stages of breath control and their benefits within the *Yoga Sutras.* One method is described as expelling air through the nostrils with 'special effort', then lengthening the amount of time between breaths, so as to eventually reach a state whereby the cessation of both inhaling and exhaling can be sustained for a long period of time. The practice of pranayama has developed and evolved since the composition of the *Yoga Sutras* and has gained much scientific interest in recent times for the physical and mental health benefits it offers.

Chanting and Mantras

Along with the physical postures of Yoga, chanting mantras (the repetition of sacred words or vows) is encouraged, with the aim of fixing the mind on ideals which pertain towards Moksha.

The *Bhagavad Gita* describes the chanting practice:

> ***One who is engaged in the practice of concentration, uttering the monosyllable Om (the Brahman or consciousness) who remembers it always, he attains the supreme goal***
> ***(Bhagavad Gita, 8.13)***

The practice of chanting is thought to serve the purpose of focusing the mind from distraction and lower mind states, as well as providing healing. Mantras are given as one technique for achieving 'mystic skills' and subtle higher states of consciousness.

They are popular as they mimic prayer, and only require vocal cords working as opposed to the physical postures which require more fitness. Many mantras have been passed down over millennia in keeping with the oral tradition.

A common mantra is simply chanting Om, for many repetitions.

Inner Discipline

When one plane has been conquered by samyama, it is applied to the next immediately following. No one who has not conquered the lower plane can jump over the plane immediately following, and then achieve samyama with reference to the plane further off
(Yoga Sutra, 3.6 (Commentary by Vsaya))

Samyama is a term which roughly translates to 'inner discipline'. This refers to the integration of the three final limbs of Yoga listed as above: 'concentration', 'meditation', and 'absorption'. These three limbs progress step by step, towards the goal of ultimate freedom. Each of these limbs can seem quite similar at first, so it is important to explore the concept further. Ultimately, the *Yoga Sutra* is an instruction manual, with the eight limbs given as tools for liberation, and discipline is needed to follow these instructions and cast aside distractions.

Imagine sitting in front of a tree in an empty field.

1. Concentration of your attention in a steadfast manner onto that tree, free from distraction.

2. Continuation of this method of concentration, to further reflect (for example, how a tree is one entity, but also a composite of many smaller entities, or how the tree is both part of and separate from the field, or how the tree is both alive, and mortal) may be understood as meditation.

3. Then to go further and no longer reflect on the properties of the tree, and to lose your sense of self, and to become 'one' with the tree, and all it is connected to, Is understood as absorption , or 'oneness'.

These three 'steps' of levels of awareness, follow on from one another, and are together understood as the 'inner discipline'.

God

From Devotion To God, Samadhi Is Attained.
(Yoga Sutra, 2.45)

There is an undeniably religious aspect to Yoga, which in keeping with the orthodox Hindu position believes in a supreme deity. This deity sustains the universe and is both outside of it and within it. It is called Brahman. Yoga recognises that the responsibility is on one's self however to reach salvation through practice. Rather than by appealing to God for pure salvation, they invoke the idea of God to help their practice. Much of yogic practice is developed around devotion.

Conclusion

Yoga is a practical philosophy that relies on a framework and many key concepts from the Hindu tradition, most notably the Samkhya school.

The Yoga Sutra written by Patañjali is the key text, although the Yoga school believes in the authority of the *Vedas* and the *Bhagavad Gita* amongst other Hindu texts.

Yoga is an instruction of practical steps that can be taken to achieve the 'ultimate freedom', (Moksha) which is to release the soul from the cycle of rebirth. The focus is on postures, chanting, mantras, abstentions and meditation to achieve the highest state of mind: 'Samdhi', which precedes Moksha.

Yoga relies on a world view that claims the human condition is unsatisfactory in some sense, and so must be transcended. The cycle of reincarnation is caused by the bond of Purusa and Prakriti and so the goal of Yoga is to break this bond, and free the consciousness from the material world of nature. The Yoga Sutra sets forth the 'eight limbs of Yoga', as a structured path towards liberation.

Chapter 3:

BUDDHISM

Buddhism is both a major world religion and a system of ideas, or philosophy. Unlike most other religions, Buddhism does not focus on belief in a God or creator and instead places emphasis on the goal to achieve 'freedom from suffering' or *Nirvana*. This goal of Buddhism is arrived at via what is called the Noble Eightfold path. It is considered one of the 'Heterodox' schools of Indian philosophy, as it rejects the ultimate authority of the *Vedas* (whilst still drawing from the Vedic tradition).

There is debate as to whether Buddhism can be truly labelled a religion, due a lack of focus on a creator. That depends on definitions. In practice, it carries many of the features of religion. Over the past two and a half thousand years Buddhism has spread across Asia and the rest of the world, developing various sects and incorporating elements of local cultures and religions wherever it has settled. More recently Buddhism has become popular in the Western world. Here we will focus on the core concepts behind the original teachings, which are the foundations for Buddhism in any form.

Buddhism was founded by Siddhartha Gautama, who was born in modern day Nepal in 480 BC. He was raised as a prince, indulging in the riches of royalty and abundance. As a young man, yearning for meaning, he escaped his life of material wealth and spent years living with severely strict monks who believed in depriving themselves of worldly pleasures as a route to enlightenment. It is said that Siddhartha starved himself to the edge of death but became disillusioned when he realised such extreme practises had not led to his desire of enlightenment.

Soon after, when meditating under a Bodhi tree, he had a sudden realisation that there is a 'middle way' between decadence and poverty, and this 'middle way' became a fundamental theme of Buddhism. Siddrartha would have been steeped in the Vedic ideas explored in the Yoga and Nyaya chapters, and so in one sense Buddhism can be understood as a reformation of Vedic and Hindu soteriology.

The age of Siddhartha (563-483 BC) was a time of philosophical revolution in India. For thousands of years prior, the Vedic systems had dominated thought, with an increasingly dogmatic approach which placed emphasis on a class and priest system of top-down scholarship. Although Buddhism may now seem ancient, at its birth it was a revolutionary system of ideas, presenting a direct challenge to the religious dogma of the day.

Siddhartha taught his ideas in Pali, which was the 'common' language of his time, which was in itself a revolutionary act. Previously Sanskrit was used, which limited understanding to the priestly classes. This can be compared to Lutheran Churches daring to teach the Bible in German or English instead of Latin 1500 years later in Europe.

Siddhartha was notable for teaching for free, and rejecting the notion that his words should be secret or codified. He wanted to spread his ideas in the simplest possible terms, so as to be easily understood and useful to everyone. His teachings were first orally transmitted and then written down into various books, or *Sutras.* His teaching became known within Buddhist circles as 'The Dharma'.

Siddhartha Guatuama became known as the 'The Buddha' in later centuries, which is roughly translated to 'enlightened one'.

The Four Noble Truths:

Siddhartha believed it was important that he shared his teachings, he believed in simplifying them as much as possible so they were accessible to all. He began by distilling his core realisations into the Four 'Noble Truths', which are:

1. All existence entails suffering.
2. Suffering is caused by craving.
3. Eliminating craving eliminates suffering.
4. There is a path to eliminating suffering (the Noble Eightfold Path).

Let's examine these one by one:

1. Arguing that all existence is 'suffering', may at first seem a rather negative outlook on life. However a Buddhist would argue that all life events, even initially good ones, do entail some form of suffering. For example, we may be very happy that we have money, or friends, however when we inevitably lose them, we will be sad and suffer. Can you imagine any form of existence that entails no suffering at all? Different lives will have different amounts of suffering, but according to Siddhartha, all life does entail suffering to an extent.

2. Siddhartha believed that craving or desire is the cause of suffering for a number of reasons. Craving causes us to place focus on satisfaction from external factors, which are subject to change and decay. By craving outcomes, we cannot live fully in the present. Craving will lead to unhappiness because we will either not get what we crave, and be unhappy, or achieve it and then inevi-

tably lose it (as all things are subject to change) and then be unhappy again.

3. Therefore, based on the above, if we can eliminate craving, we can eliminate suffering.

4. The above principles may at first glance seem negative, however the fourth noble truth offers hope, a roadmap to eliminate craving and suffering- this is the Noble Eightfold Path.

The Noble Eightfold Path:

The Noble Eightfold Path is a list of eight 'right' behaviours. These are not to be understood as 'laws' or strict rules. They are simple directions for living, that Siddhartha taught if one follows, one can eliminate suffering and reach Nirvana. They are:

1. Right View
2. Right Intention
3. Right Speech
4. Right Conduct
5. Right Livelihood
6. Right Effort
7. Right Mindfulness
8. Right Meditation

Let's examine one by one, with examples from Buddhist texts:

1. **Right view** is the first and foundational principle that supports all the others. Right view is understood as a correct insight into key principles of Buddhist thought (such as impermanence, suffering, rebirth, non-self) which we discuss in more detail below, and an understanding of the Four Noble Truths. It is where one must begin.

"And what is right view? Knowledge with regard to suffering, knowledge with regard to the origination of suffering, knowledge with regard to the cessation of suffering, knowledge with regard to the way of practice leading to the cessation of suffering: This is called right view."
(Maha-satipatthana Sutta: DN:22)

2. **Right intention** is a key principle of Buddhist ethics, and guides us to act with compassion (do no harm) and non-attachment as our principles toward life and others. Note that intention of actions, not their outcomes, is the focus of Buddhist morality.

Aspiring to renunciation, to freedom from ill will, to harmlessness: This is called right intention.
(Maha-satipatthana Sutta: DN:22)

3. **Right speech** is understood as no lying, gossip, slander or to refrain from any speech which causes suffering to yourself or others.

Never speak harsh words
For they will rebound upon you.
(Dhammapada, 10)

4. **Right conduct** is understood as no violence, killing or stealing.

> ***If you kill, lie or steal...***
> ***You dig up your own roots.***
> ***(Dhammapada,18)***

5. **Right livelihood** is the idea that one should try to make their living in a way which harms others as little as possible and is consistent with 1, 2, 3 and 4.

> ***"A lay follower should not engage in five types of business. Which five? Business in weapons, business in human beings, business in meat, business in intoxicants, and business in poison."***
> ***(Vanijja Sutta, AN 5.177)***

6. **Right effort** is understood as guarding the mind against unwholesome states- which can be done through stages 7 and 8 (note that the Buddha acknowledged that his teachings took effort and focus to put into practice, and are not just an easy 'ticket' to a better life). It is also the general attitude of putting effort into all the other points of the path. Siddhartha knew it took resolve.

> ***It is you who must make the effort.***
> ***The masters only point the way.***
> ***(Dhammapada, 20)***

7. **Right mindfulness** is to live in freedom from desire and uneasy mental states, and to appreciate the impermanent nature of the body, emotions, and mental states.

"...where a monk remains focused on the body in & of itself — ardent, alert, & mindful — putting aside greed & distress...He remains focused on feelings in & of themselves... the mind in & of itself... This is called right mindfulness..." (Maha-satipatthana Sutta: DN:22)

8. **Right concentration** is when one is free of lust, desire and wrong view, and dwells in a state of extreme contentment that comes from observing the eightfold path. Siddhartha describes an esoteric fivefold process which is quite detailed. Essentially though it is a subtle and refined state of mind which results from observing the previous steps in the path.

Any singleness of mind equipped with these seven factors — right view, right resolve, right speech, right action, right livelihood, right effort, & right mindfulness — is called noble right concentration (Maha-cattarisaka Sutta: MN 117)

These teachings are taken together, and rely on each to stand as a complete structure. Siddhartha laid them out in as simple terms as possible, and importantly he argued that anyone, man or woman, young or old, rich or poor, could follow these teachings and receive the benefits. This was a revolutionary idea in a time when religious and spiritual teachings were the domain of a priestly class, and enlightenment was often assumed to be a right for those born into privileged positions.

The Three Basic Facts of Existence:

Beyond the Eightfold path, the Buddha posited three 'basic facts of existence' which form the basis of 'Right View'.

1. **Impermanence**
2. **Suffering**
3. **Non-self**

Impermanence

This is the idea that all things are subject to change, with no exception. Impermanence informs many other Buddhist ideas.

It is used to motivate a sense of detachment and to explain our delusions which cause suffering. An example of a delusional view may be that a young and fit body will last forever, when this inevitably begins to age and change it causes suffering based on your wrong view that your body would be fixed to one state. By this same notion, recognition of impermanence can provide us with detachment from our delusions and a sense of ease of what is to come.

Impermanence is also used to motivate our own behaviour towards a superior morality and more harmonious relationship with life. As life is short, why would we waste it arguing or in moral neglect?

You too shall pass away. Knowing this, how can you quarrel? How easily the wind overturns a frail tree.
(Dhammapada, 7)

...it remains a fact that the fixed and necessary constitution of being that all constituents are transitory. (Anguttara-Nikâya, 3.134)

The Buddhist view of Impermanence goes further than the orthodox Hindu schools, and argues that even the non-material elements of life (such as soul, consciousness & 'self') are transitory. It could be said that Buddhism prescribes the 'ultimate' version of impermanence. This total impermanence worldview informs all aspects of Buddhist thought, from epistemology to ontology.

Suffering (Dukkha)

Whilst effort is made here to use the best English translations, the Pali word *Dukkha* deserves some attention. *Dukkha* has many potential English translations which generally describe a negative mental state in one way or another. Suffering is a broad term to cover these but may not deliver the nuance of the phrase. In different contexts Dukkha can be translated as 'un-satisfactoriness', 'stress' 'anxiety', 'pain', 'despair' 'separation from a loved one', or 'sorrow'. These are all forms of *Dukkha*. Many of the symptoms of various mental illnesses such as low mood, mania, psychosis, depression, may also be described as *Dukkha*. If Buddhism is said to have one clear theme, it is centred around escaping *Dukkha*.

"Both formerly & now, it is only Dukkha that I describe, and the cessation of dukkha." (Anuradha Sutta, 22.86)

The idea that painful mental states which involve suffering are tied to our existence was the fundamental problem which

Siddhartha wanted to solve. Rather than being pessimistic, his teachings are an attempt at a solution. Siddhartha argued that to solve the problem of suffering, we first had to acknowledge it as a basic fact of existence. We have to face the problem head on.

Non-Self

When we come to examine the elements of being one by one, we discover that in the absolute sense there is no living entity there to form a basis for such figments as "I am". (Visuddhi-Magga, chap. Xviii)

The third basic fact of existence is described as 'non-self'. The Buddha taught that all things are subject to change and impermanence, and this even includes the 'self'.

This can be a difficult concept to grasp, especially to the Western mind which has grown up in a society which places emphasis on the self as a concrete idea.

Siddhartha taught that we are made up of sensory components, such as sight, smell, touch, taste etc. and that our sense of self is the sum total of these components. But it is just that, a sense or illusion and not a real thing.

Siddhartha gave the example of a chariot (we will use a car) to demonstrate how this concept of non-self-works.

His argument was that just as a car is a useful concept; it is in fact just the sum total of many separate parts. This is why the idea is 'non-self', instead of 'not-self'. He was not denying that a car exists as a concept- it does, and it has a use. But when we examine it more closely, we may realise it is an 'empty' concept.

A car, just as the idea of self, is really just a composite of many different parts. A car has seats, wheels, an engine, a boot, a metal body, which of these parts makes up the car? Would it still be a car if each part was removed? 'Car' is really just a useful concept to think of an amalgamation of these parts into a functioning unit which can transport you. In the same way, the Buddha argued that 'self' or 'I am' is just a grouping together of various sensory components which form our consciousness for a limited time.

We could apply this same idea on a more micro level to a single component of the car. For example, an engine is a useful concept. But it is in fact just a composite of a spark, cylinder, valve and piston etc. (and then each of these is made up of smaller parts ad infinitum...). Or we could apply it at a macro level, a traffic jam is a useful way of thinking about what is in fact a mass of different cars…

Siddhartha argued then that the idea of self is similar in this sense to that of a chariot or car. Yes, we do experience our current self as one cohesive unity, and it has value and merit in that sense. However, it is a temporary coming together of our senses and faculties, which can be broken down into constituent parts.

This teaching was a bold step away from the concept of 'Atman' in the orthodox Hindu schools, and left the Buddhists with a problem of how they could argue Karma continues between lifetimes without a consistent, solid self to be bound to. This problem occupies a back and forth between Hindu and Buddhist scholars to this day and is one of the key differences between them.

It is also worth noting that Siddhartha regarded the notion of self, other, and self-identification to be associated with attachment and clinging, which as discussed is a cause of suffering.

The Middle Way

The Middle Way is key to Buddhist thought, understood as a balance between extremes. Siddhartha was raised as a prince, living a life of luxury, and as a young man decided to explore beyond the bounds of his palace. He then spent over six years living in the opposite condition of extreme abstinence and poverty. He became emaciated and gaunt in his attempts to reach spiritual salvation through deprivation.

Following these two extremes, Siddhartha, through reflecting on his lived experience in meditation, realised that there is a middle way in all things, which can be used as a guide in all situations.

Therefore, Buddhists do not deem it necessary to deprive yourself of comforts, nor to indulge in extreme luxury to escape suffering. Instead correct moderation and proper understanding of the facts of existence are seen as the key to a happier, healthier existence and ultimately, liberation. Extremes are seen as distractions.

The idea of the Middle Way can be demonstrated in relation to the sixth principle of the Noble Eightfold Path- right effort. Siddhartha argued that right effort is a balance between not enough effort, which can lead to lethargy and stagnation, and putting in too much effort, which can lead to anxiety and exhaustion.

He gave us the example of a string on a lute, that will break if strung too tight and not play a tune if too loose- this can be seen as an analogy for how we should apply our effort.

'If energy is applied too strongly, it will lead to restlessness, and if energy is too lax, it will lead to lassitude.' (Anguttara Nikaya, 6.55)

As with all other core Buddhist teachings, the Middle Way is but a means to an end of reducing suffering. In fact, the entire Noble Eightfold Path can be viewed as modes of the 'Middle Way' of living, and each point in it can be seen as a balance between two extremes.

That is the middle way, the Noble Eightfold Path, which "gives rise to vision, gives rise to knowledge, and leads to peace, to direct knowledge, to enlightenment, to Nirvana." (Samyutta Nikaya, 56:11)

Meditation

Always mindful, he breathes in; mindful he breathes out. (Digha Nikaya, 22)

Meditation is a practice, rather than an idea or theory. However, it is so central to Buddhist philosophy and the ultimate goal of *Nirvana*, that it is worth examining further.

Meditation can generally be understood as a mental practice of attention, awareness or focus, within a context of rest and composure. One of the aims of meditation is to allow for a state of 'non-reactive awareness', where one witnesses and pays attention to the activity of the mind but does not judge or react to it. Siddhartha maintained that by focusing attention on different aspects of the body and physical form, one could gain a sense of awareness and detachment from them.

The monk remains focused on the body in and of itself — ardent, alert, and mindful — putting aside greed and distress with reference to the world. (Digha Nikaya, 22)

Meditation can take many forms and objects of focus. Siddhartha encouraged meditation on each aspect of the Noble Eightfold Path to re-enforce right view. For example, meditating on impermanence by imagining the body breaking down, or meditating on right speech by visualising the negative impacts of wrong speech. Meditating to cultivate compassion for other living things is also a common Buddhist practice.

A simple way to experience and understand what basic meditation feels like is to sit in a comfortable posture, in a quiet and safe place, and focus on your diaphragm, as you breathe in and out for a few minutes. To imagine you breathe in to the diaphragm, and release tension in the area as you breathe out.

It was in meditation that the Buddha was said to have received his great enlightenment of the Middle Way, and the nature of reality. Meditation is a calm state, but it does take effort and discipline to engage in the practice regularly. The Buddha acknowledged this with the teaching of 'Right effort'.

Meditation was of course, not invented by Siddhartha, who would have learned the practice through his immersion in the

Hindu or Jain schools. Over hundreds of years Buddhist meditation took on a unique form, however it is still linked to the previous Indian traditions.

Karma and Ethics

The concept of *Karma* is another key idea which continues from the Hindu schools into Buddhism, with some differences in how it is applied. The word means 'action' in Sanskrit, and at its most basic sense Siddhartha taught that action has consequences, or 'bears fruit'.

Siddhartha taught that there are three types of action that can bear fruit- bodily, physical and mental. He taught however that it is not the action itself which bears fruit, but the intention of the action. Intention is crucial to Buddhist ethics, rather than the outcome of an action.

For example, if one said something to another person which was genuinely intended to be compassionate, however was taken as offence in another, this action would not be seen as immoral. The mental state of the agent is key in Buddhist ethics. If one acts without clinging or desire, and with the right intentions, then their action can be viewed as morally pure even if the outcome appears undesirable.

The opposite holds true. For example, if you gave someone a gift, and it made them happy, this on the face of it is a moral action. However, if your intention was to gain money (or other benefit) from them in the future, and that is the reason for the gift, then your action is muddied by an impure mental state of clinging to the concept of your own personal gain.

Siddhartha taught that Karma is non-linear, and can take a short or long time to manifest. Meaning that if you perform a negative action, it is not necessarily that the fruit of that action will ripen straight afterwards. It could be the next day, the next year or even the next life. This is one of the main issues Hindu schools have with the Buddhists, as they argue it is impossible for Karma to be applied in future rebirths if there is no 'self' or soul for it to 'cling' to.

Siddhartha argued that if one performs an action, with no mental clinging and pure intent, then their action will reap no fruit. However if we act with impure intention or clinging, we create more action (Karma) which results in further rebirth. This contributes to the endless cycle of existence.

Interdependence

> ***"this being that comes to be;***
> ***from the arising of this, that arises;***
> ***from the ceasing of this that ceases."***
> ***(Nidana Samyutta, s.11.28)***

Siddhartha argued that all aspects of reality are dependent upon each other, and there is no true separation between them. Nothing exists apart from everything else. We can understand this by imaging two realities, one which is our everyday reality, which we use for functioning and the other which is the 'ultimate reality', through which we can understand interdependence.

For example, in the 'normal' reality we live in day to day, a cup of water on a table is quite a straightforward concept. However, when viewed through the lens of the Buddhist 'ultimate' reality, we may see that the cup itself (just as the car example) is just a combination of atoms and molecules, shaped temporarily into the form of a cup. Likewise, the water is not one object, but a temporary form of molecules, which depend on the cup for their form, and for infinite previous causes to be in the place they are (river, rain, ocean etc...).

The cup and the water are dependent on each other, to form the 'cup of water', just as they are dependent on the table to hold them, which is in turn dependent on infinite other conditions. As such, every atom, form, emotion and object in the universe, is dependent on every other atom for its present form and condition, making all things interdependent, and nothing apart from everything else.

> ***From birth as a requisite condition comes ageing & death...***
> ***(Paccaya Sutta, 12.20)***

Siddhartha also used interdependence to explain life and death, arguing that they are dependent on each other, and part of the same overall reality. This is just one way in which this teaching can help to reduce suffering.

Rebirth

Rebirth is a concept which at first glance is an acceptance of the Hindu position on reincarnation, which Siddhartha would have been taught in his early life. However, there are differences. As mentioned, the Buddhists have no concept of a permanent 'self' which reincarnates.

It is crucial to have an understanding of rebirth, if one is to understand the Three Basic Facts of Existence in their proper context.

Siddhartha taught that human life was unique and an extremely rare opportunity to achieve Nirvana. He denied that this could be done in either the low states of existence (animals or plants) or the higher states of existence (Devas/gods). This relates back to the Middle Way. He argued that human existence in itself could be a form of 'middle path', in which we have the right combination of suffering, pleasure, and intellect to realise the Four Noble Truths and liberate ourselves.

Siddhartha argued that there are realms of existence below and above human life. Many are lower realms which involve huge amounts of suffering. Here the suffering is so intense that one does not have the tools or time to consider the Buddhist teachings. Then there are the higher realms in which the pleasure is so intense that one is trapped in clinging to it. However, these realms, and all realms, exist within the context of impermanence. So, neither a hell of a heaven realm lasts forever. The *Karma* will eventually be used up and lead to new births.

Siddhartha spoke of 'rebirth' rather than 'reincarnation'. For Buddhists, there is no fixed 'soul' or person which travels between lives, there is however a continuous thread of consciousness. This thread may be imagined as a car which changes each part day by day, until there is nothing left of the original car. There is nothing solid of the original car left, due to impermanence of all things, however the continuous thread of a 'car' has maintained.

Generosity and Compassion

> ***If beings knew, as I know,***
> ***the results of giving & sharing,***
> ***they would not eat without having given,***
> ***nor would the stain of miserliness***
> ***overcome their minds.***
> ***(Itivuttaka, 1.26)***

Siddhartha argued that generosity to others and compassion for living things were crucial elements to becoming liberated from suffering. Compassion was Siddhartha's antidote to desire and clinging. He thought that everyone is equal in their ability to suffer, and developed his philosophy of liberation as an act of compassion for others so they could be free from it.

> ***The fool laughs at generosity... the master finds joy in giving and happiness is his reward. (Dhammapada, 177)***

Ontology:

> ***Form is Emptiness, Emptiness is Form. (Heart Sutra, verse 3)***

Buddhist Ontology is similar in some regards to the orthodox Hindu schools (of course it was founded in their footsteps) however with some very key differences. Concepts such as *Karma*, *Samsara*, and rebirth are similar.

However, a key difference is that Buddhists reject permanence in any form, so there is no room for eternal substances (such as souls or atoms), universals are rejected, and ultimately all things are regarded as empty at their core.

The idea of 'Emptiness' does not necessarily mean that there is 'nothing there'. Instead, it refers to the fact that all concepts are just temporary forms, subject to interdependence, impermanence and infinite division. When you break down anything into its constituent temporary parts, this process can be done infinitely.

Therefore, from a Buddhist perspective, there is no unchanging 'substrate' to reality such as atoms, because ultimately all things (even atoms) can be broken down into nothingness. Therefore, whilst concepts are useful in everyday terms (e.g., table, person, atom) when analysed in view of the 'ultimate reality', they are empty.

This carries over into the Buddhist view of ethics. Whilst saying an action is right or wrong has utility, there is no ultimate 'good', 'bad', 'pure' or 'impure' in the Buddhist context, these ideas too are ultimately empty for a Buddhist.

> ***"...feeling, perception, formation, and consciousness are emptiness.... There is no impurity and no purity..."***
> ***(Heart Sutra, verse 3)***

As with all other fixed and permanent concepts, the Buddhists reject the notion of universals as described in the Nyaya chapter. They instead argued that universals are just useful names and not real. This view has become known as nominalism.

The Buddhists also rejected the direct realism of the Nyaya and Vaisheshika schools (discussed in the next chapter), as well as the dualism of the Samkhya and Yoga schools.

The Buddhists argue that the reality we perceive is dependent on our mind, and vice versa. This is known as a form of idealism.

For consider the world- a bubble, a mirage. See the world as it is, and death will overlook you. (Dhammapada, 171)

Summary:

Buddhist philosophy is a system which exists with the ultimate aim of liberating humans from suffering. It grew from the Vedic and Hindu culture, but eventually rejected many of the orthodoxies of those schools, and developed its own soteriology.

Some of the key aspects which differentiate it from orthodox Hindus Schools are: rejection of a permanent soul or consciousness, the theory of 'non-self', an idealist view of reality, and less of a reliance on God or a creator.

This system of ideas was the work of Siddhartha, a prince who grew up in a Vedic society, and then lived a life of deprivation- leading him to find balance and argue for the 'Middle Way'. He came to be known as 'the Buddha'.

The core principles of Buddhism can be refined to: The Four Noble Truths, the Noble Eightfold path, and the Three Basic Facts of Existence.

The Four Noble Truths argue that all life is suffering. Suffering is caused by craving and desire, but crucially there is a way to escape this:

The Noble Eightfold Path is an eight-point guide to behaviour and conduct which can liberate us from suffering by eliminating our clinging and desire.

Crucial to the Noble Eightfold Path is a proper understanding of the three facts of existence: impermanence, suffering, and non-self.

Meditation is a necessary tool for achieving proper understanding of the Three Basic Facts of existence, and liberation from suffering

Buddhists reject the notion of self, or a soul, or any permanent thing for that matter. They believe that all concepts are inherently empty.

Key Texts:

Buddhism, as a religion as well as a philosophy, has many important texts.

Pali Canon

The most fundamental perhaps is the Pali Canon, which is a large compilation of speeches and talks given by the Buddha to his followers, it is known as the "word of the Buddha". Most of the books in this compilation take the form of the Buddha explaining his position through repetition and examples, to his monks, including their questioning. This is likely to have been written down a few hundred years after his death, after having been memorised. The Pali Canon can be categorised into three 'baskets' or sections:

- *The Vinaya Pitaka* (Discipline basket)
- *Sutta Pitaka* (Sayings basket)
- *Abhidhamma Pitaka* (Philosophy basket)

Dhammapada

The *Dhammapada* is a concise collection of Buddhist sayings and teachings, broken down into twenty six chapters. It is quite poetic in nature, and more descriptive than philosophical. If you want to capture the essence of Buddhism and its teachings in one book, this is probably the best place to start. The *Dhammapada* is just one small section of the entire Pali Canon. There are many translations available, some more poetic, like that of Thomas Byrom, and some truer to the original Pali, like that of Thanissaro Bhikkhu.

Chapter 4:

NYAYA

न्याय

Nyaya is a one of the six major schools of Hindu philosophy, Its genesis is dated roughly to 550 BC. Nyaya is an orthodox school and as such argues for the traditional Hindu concepts such as the soul (Atman), a creator deity (Brahman), and the law of action and reaction (Karma). Like all other Hindu schools, Nyaya shares the fundamental goal of liberating the soul from the cycle of reincarnation (Samsara).

However Nyaya philosophers are unique in that they focused on knowledge as the primary means of liberation, rather than postures, moral actions, or worship. Therefore epistemology and logic are particularly important to the Nyaya as it is their basis for liberation.

Nyaya believes in the authority of the *Vedas* and defends the classic beliefs of orthodox schools. As such, the Nyaya contributed significantly to the development of Indian philosophy as a whole, which is why they are included in this book.

The defining text is the *Nyaya Sutra*, ascribed to an ancient scholar called Aksapāda Gautama and is thought to have been written sometime between the 6th century BCE and the 2nd century AD. The text is composed of five books, each with two chapters, with a focus on epistemology, metaphysics and logic.

In India it was common for two schools to group together over time, and borrow or share parts of their world-view with each other. In a similar way, Nyaya is closely related to another Hindu school called *Vaisesika* and they share many core beliefs. Some would argue that they merged into one metaphysical framework.

Traditionally the Nyaya school was more concerned with epistemology and logic, and the Vaisesika with metaphysics and ontology. This chapter will focus on Nyaya and the beliefs they incorporated from the Vaisesika school, and group them together.

The Nyaya developed a complex system of epistemology and logic throughout the years, with many of the developments spurred on by the ongoing disputes with other schools (e.g. the Buddhists). This is typical of Hindu schools, who refined themselves over centuries by debating each other on core issues such as epistemology, the nature of reality, the existence of God, and the self.

The Nyaya school spent a great deal of attention in defining different types of perception. They also regarded logic as a core interest, and are famous for their response to the problem of induction. The name Nyaya translates roughly to 'method, logic, or mind led to conclusion', so evidently the school is associated with analytic thinking and debate.

Nyaya is a realist school, meaning that they believe objects in the world really do exist, regardless of whether someone is observing them or not. They also believe and argue for the existence of a real eternal 'self' (Atman). They believe that perception is a valid source of knowledge, and we can know the world around us via our senses. This may seem fairly straightforward, but in some regards was a bold defence of common sense principles compared to other schools.

They advocated an idea known as 'atomism'. They believed that nature is made of fundamental, irreducible and eternal 'building block' components that form together to make substances. Hundreds of years before microscopes or modern science, this was a radical proposition.

What sets the Nyaya apart from other Hindu schools is their focus on epistemology and logic, and their belief that orthodox Hindu concepts such as a creator God, and a self or soul (Atman) were not just self evident, but needed detailed arguments to defend them. Many of these arguments pre date similar arguments in Western philosophy, and laid the groundwork for future generations of philosophers across Asia and Europe.

The Nyaya School believed in the process of debate, and reaching conclusions via hearing both sides of an argument.

Ascertainment is the removal of doubt, and the determination of a question, by hearing two opposite sides. (Nyaya Sutra, 1.1.41)

Epistemology, Perception and Properties.

Perception, inference, comparison, and word (verbal testimony)- these are the means of right knowledge. (Nyaya Sutra, 2.1.3)

The Nyaya (like other Hindu schools) believed that human souls are trapped into the 'bondage' of rebirth in this world (and other worlds), in an infinite round of birth and death. The idea of the self or soul (Atman), is crucial here. As there needs to be some sort of permanent 'self' which exists between lives. The key difference between Nyaya and other Hindu schools here, is the reason given for the bondage to the cycle of rebirth.

Whilst other schools argue it is desire, or moral shortcomings, or Karma, the Nyaya school argues that the fundamental reason for this bondage is false knowledge. Therefore discovering what is true, and rejecting what is false, was of vital importance.

Epistemology often contains reference to logic, perception, testimony and other common sources of how we gain understanding of the world. For the Nyaya, knowledge is regarded as something you 'do', an activity you participate in to liberate your soul from suffering, rather than something you just gain or come to by chance.

Perception

Perception is that knowledge which arises from the contact of a sense with its object and which is determinate, unnameable and non-erratic. (Nyaya Sutra, 2.1.4)

The Nyaya school may be described by Western philosophers as a 'Direct Realist' school. This means that they believe that objects really do 'exist' in the external world, and have their own reality and properties independent of human perception. This position put the Nyaya school at direct odds with the Buddhists and the other Hindu schools.

For example, take a wooden table in a garden. The Nyaya argue that this table exists in the garden, regardless of whether someone is there looking at it or not. That may seem fairly uncontroversial. The Nyaya go further, and claim that the properties of the table (e.g. 'woodenness', the smooth texture, deep brown colour, oak smell) exist within the table. These properties may be perceived by a human, but the property is not a result of the human perception, it is just observed by them.

Someone might argue that the property of 'brownness' (the colour of the table) cannot be a property inherent in the table, as the colour brown is perceived by the human eye and brain, and known to a human as a certain colour. The Nyaya would argue that the property brown very much exists within the table, as the potential to stimulate the sense of 'brown' within a person.

The age old philosophical question 'If a tree fell in the woods and there was no one there to hear it, would it make a sound?', could be answered quite simply from the Nyaya perspective- yes.

Well, they would assert that the sound is a property of the action of the tree falling, and not dependent on someone perceiving it for it to exist. The Nyaya believe that objects and their properties exist whether or not they are being observed. The sound of the crashing tree would be a property of the action of the tree falling, which whilst it could be perceived by a human, would exist as a result of the action rather than a result of it being perceived.

The Nyaya go as far as to argue that only direct perception can be classified as true knowledge. For example, they believed that memory is not a reliable source of knowledge, as it is only a representation of direct perception, and therefore is subject to error. Therefore they are reluctant to rely on memory as a source of knowledge.

Perception

Perception, and the senses which are used to perceive, are then very important to Nyaya epistemology.

They lay out four conditions of something being perceived as perceptual:

1. That a direct connection exists between an exterior object, and the sense organ perceiving it.

2. This connection is not understood via or interrupted via language. For example, seeing a giraffe before your brain registers the term 'giraffe'. This is important as it serves to distinguish between direct perception, and conditioned thoughts or testimony.

3. The object one is sensing is not a hallucination or delusion. (The Nyaya acknowledge that these do exist), for example seeing a mirage of water in the road.

4. The object is not 'doubtful'. Similar to point 3, this deals with 'false' perceptions, but also contains dubious categories of one cannot be sure. e.g. seeing what you think is a shadow in the distance and being unsure if it is a human shadow, or just a pattern in the trees.

The Nyaya school does also allow for perception to be valid via some more mystical sources such as meditation and experience of 'universals' (to be discussed further).

This may be curious to a Western mind, that a school so seemingly sceptical that they would lay out foundations for what can be qualified as perception, would accept that knowledge can be obtained through mystical means.

We must remember that the Nyaya are an orthodox Hindu school, who accept the authority of the *Vedas* and traditional non physical concepts such as the soul, rebirth and existence of God. Whilst they are a realist school, they certainly are not reductionist materialists in the mould of modern Western science.

Nyaya dismissed sceptical schools such as the Buddhists, who argue that we cannot be sure of the difference between false and real perceptions and therefore the nature of the external world. They argued that false perceptions are imitations of real ones (e.g. a tree can only be called a mirage if there is a real tree in the world). To the Nyaya, calling something a false perception is a clear indication that true perceptions exist as an alternative to that, therefore it is our job to define what is true and real.

Testimony

> ***Word (verbal testimony) is the instructive assertion of a reliable person.***
> ***(Nyaya Sutra, 1.1.7)***

Testimony is important for the Nyaya, who regard it as a necessary tool of knowledge. The *Nyaya Sutra* spends a fair amount of time going back and forth on arguments regarding testimony, ultimately deciding that it must be a reliable source of knowledge (on the condition that the one giving testimony can be deemed reliable). It would be unacceptable to imagine that all testimony could be deemed unreliable, that would lead to a world where one could only gain knowledge they had come to themselves and not be able to learn at all from others or from reading, which would severely limit the scope of what can be called knowledge.

The Nyaya argue for the authority of the Vedas, denying that they are contradictory by invoking the reliability of the authors. This is a demonstration of their use of testimony as a form of knowledge, and evidence that testimony is important to orthodox Hindus if they are to argue for the authority of the Vedas.

> ***'The Veda is reliable...like medical science, because of the reliability of the authors' (Nyaya Sutra, 2.1.69)***

Atoms, Properties and qualities

The Nyaya school developed a detailed system of 'atoms', 'substances', 'qualities' 'properties' and 'universals' to categorise different types of objects and their various aspects. This is partly due to their direct realism, meaning that they needed to justify the existence of objects as separate from the human mind and how they operate in the world. Many of these concepts developed by the Nyaya are similar to concepts used much later in Western philosophy and as with the rest of the Nyaya theory, it is worth bearing in mind that these concepts were developed long before modern science and in line with a traditional understanding of Hindu metaphysics and ontology.

Atoms

> ***An atom, on the other hand, is eternal though not intangible. (Nyaya Sutra, 2.2.25)***

The Nyaya school is atomistic, meaning that they believe all physical nature can be broken down into fundamental, indivisible building blocks. The atomism of the Nyaya relied on their acceptance of their being five core 'elements' which all things partake in, which are listed as: earth, water, fire, air, and 'upper space'.

These five types of atoms make up all known physical objects. Atoms are said to be eternal and therefore cannot be changed or destroyed. (This is a direct challenge to the Buddhist world-view that everything is impermanent).

They gave one particular argument (amongst others) for the existence of atoms and responded to counter arguments from rival schools over the years. The existence of atoms is important to their entire ontology, so it was important for them to define and defend the idea.

The argument goes like this:

All visible objects are composed of parts that we can see, therefore the smallest parts we can see must be composed of even smaller parts we cannot see. This cannot go on forever otherwise It would cause infinite division (which is impossible) therefore there must be a thing which cannot be parted and is indivisible, which are the smallest thing- these must be the atoms.

Rival schools responded to this argument by asking "why is infinite division impossible?" Perhaps it is possible and therefore there would be no need for the existence of an indivisible fundamental such as an atom.

The Nyaya commonly responded by comparing two different sized objects. For example if we take an ant and a tree. They are vastly different in size. However if infinite division is possible then both would have the same amount of 'parts' (infinite), which would mean it wouldn't make sense to define them as a different size. The Nyaya school argued that surely the tree has more 'parts' than the ant and this is a common sense approach to the nature of reality. Therefore infinite division is impossible in their world view.

Nyaya held that two atoms of the same type could join together and create what is called a dyad, and three of the same type would form a triad. The triads of atoms of a particular type were said to be the smallest object one could perceive.

So, the Nyaya believe that all things in the universe are made of one of five elements which are all impermanent. The elements are composed of imperceivable, indivisible atoms. The 'things' themselves are said to be impermanent and not eternal. However the atoms which are the building blocks of all elements are themselves eternal.

Substances and Qualities

Substances (Guna)

The Nyaya school argued for the existence of enduring substances. A substance is a defined type of object which itself can carry different qualities. The idea of a substance is that it has set parameters and if these are changed then it is no longer that substance. For example the substance of 'banana' has defined qualities such as 'yellowness', 'banana taste' and 'curved' or 'textured' appearance. These different qualities work together to form a substance known as banana. If we were to say the object in question did not taste of banana, have a yellow colour, or a curved shape, or skin, then we could not reasonably say it is a banana.

They believed that substances could be physical (such as bananas or countless other examples) or non physical, such as a soul.

Qualities (Dravya)

A quality is considered as a property of a substance. For example the taste, texture, and colour of a peanut. Qualities can include sensory elements as the given examples but also temporal and elements and dimensions, such as size, area, shape or weight. The main thing is that qualities can be changed, they are not permanent like substances- however if they are changed enough then they will no longer define one certain substance.

Universals

A universal is understood by the Nyaya as the non-physical, timeless, archetype of a certain substance. Think of it as an 'ideal' that exists independently of any particular example in the world. Universals exist outside of space and time, however they define substances. For example, there will be a universal 'peanut', which allows real world substances (peanuts) to 'inhere' their qualities from. This process is known as the property of 'Inherence'.

Universals are regarded as very 'real' by the Nyaya, however whilst their particulars inherit qualities from them, they exist independently of them. So if all peanuts on earth disappeared, in theory the 'universal peanut' would still exist. The object in the world is known as the 'particular'.

Although peanuts will hold slight differences in their shapes, sizes, colours, and location, the Nyaya view is that they share common qualities which they 'inherit' from the universal peanut. The same is true of all substances both living and non-living.

One purpose of universals for the Nyaya was to properly categorise different substances in the external world. They thought that without the presence of universals, then the differences between things could be minimised and lead to a breakdown of categorisation which was unacceptable for them.

Something is needed to explain the commonalities between all peanuts, or horses, that despite their differences still make them a peanut or a horse. The Nyaya explain this by arguing that horses and peanuts both inherit properties from their respective universal.

It is defined as 'an entity which is eternal and inseparably inherent in many entities'. (JIP, 1975, 3.3-4)

A Universal does not have to be an object. The Nyaya also argue that there are universals of properties, such as 'redness' (There would be a universal of the colour red) or weight, e.g. a universal of 'heavy' or even spatial proximity, e.g. a universal of 'closeness'.

The relationship between a universal and its particular is known as *Sumavaya*, and it defies the usual laws of physical relations between two physical objects. The bond between a universal and its particular is non physical, and the particular is said to be inseparable from the universal.

So, for the Nyaya, universals are non physical (but still real) entities, which hold certain qualities, from which particulars (the things in the world) inhere. Universals are used to explain the categorisations between different substances in the physical world.

Although there are infinite universals, two fundamental 'types' are said to exist:

Higher Universal- confers the property of existence on to something (e.g. peanut, horse, tree)

Lower Universals- the individual qualities which discriminate between things (e.g. size, space, colour)

Absences:

As well as substances, qualities, and universals, the Nyaya listed another category of things: 'Absences'. They recognised that the absence of something was in itself a phenomena which must be accounted for in their metaphysical framework. They defined four main types of absences:

Prior absence- the absence of something before it is caused, e.g. the absence of a calf before it is born.

Destruction- the destruction of something that exists, e.g. burning wood into ashes.

Mutual absence- the absence of mutual qualities between two different things. e.g. the calf and the wood have mutual absences of qualities between them as they are so different.

Absolute negation- this covers logical impossibilities, e.g. the statement 'no dry wood can burn', is impossible as being able to burn is a property of dry wood. Therefore the statement is a negation of basic logic.

The Problem of Induction

> ***Intellect, apprehension and knowledge, these are not different from one another.***
> ***(Nyaya Sutra, 1.1.15)***

The Nyaya school is known for attempts to solve the problem of induction, which is an ancient issue debated by philosophers across the world. The problem is usually associated with David Hume and more recent Western philosophers, however the issue has been the subject of fierce debate in Indian philosophy for at least two thousand years.

Their view on induction is best associated with a philosopher known as Gangeśa (The Great Professor). In his fourteenth century classical work *The Jewel*, he developed and argued for many of the Nyaya positions on logic and epistemology. He is considered to be one of the most important Hindu philosophers across all schools due to his contribution to logic and maths in particular.

So, What is induction, or inductive reasoning?

Inductive reasoning is a way of reaching a conclusion, in which the premise supplies some (but not all) of the evidence, and we assume the rest. For example if I see smoke, I might induce that there is some fire (as I know from my experience that there is usually combustion that causes smoke…In fact I have never seen smoke without it).

Contrast this with deductive reasoning. For example if I see smoke, and the fire below, then I can deduce that the fire caused the smoke, as I can actually see it happening, and there is no blank action to be filled in my reasoning.

The problem of induction occurs as so much of our day to day knowledge is formed by inductive reasoning, as we cannot always see every factor of a situation and so we have to use it most of the time. For example when feeding a horse carrots, we know that every other horse in our experience can eat them and likes them, so induce that they will not kill this horse or be bad for her.

This is a problem because the Nyaya want to claim that they can have knowledge from induction, rather than just 'good probability' of something being true. Remember- knowledge is everything to the Nyaya- they needed to be able to define it in order to justify their path to liberation.

The Nyaya philosopher wants to claim that they can have knowledge of a general statement like 'horses like carrots', or something even more basic like 'all horses have hooves', without having to go and examine every horse in the world, which would be impossible.

They attempt to solve this problem by appealing to a non-material type of perception. They argue that a person can experience a universal (e.g. the universal of horse) and then extract elements of it towards all the particulars in the world. So the Nyaya would argue that you could actually have knowledge that all horses like carrots, or have hoofs, just by perceiving the universal 'horse', rather than going and checking every horse in the world.

Other schools (such as the Carvaka school) have argued that there is not a need to claim induction leads to knowledge, and only deductive knowledge can be true knowledge. They would argue that there will always be an exception to a rule, for example a horse which is allergic to carrots, or born without hooves. Or to cite another example, smoke which comes not from a fire but from another uncommon source.

However this is intolerable for the Nyaya, with their realist and common sense world view. They needed to be able to claim that day to day reasoning is knowledge and not subject to doubt. If they became sceptical about inductive knowledge it would greatly reduce the potential knowledge base one could have in order to obtain liberation. Therefore it was important for them to defend it.

God

God is...the father of all beings. Who can demonstrate the existence of Him who transcends the evidences of perceptions, inference and scripture...?
(Nyaya Sutra, 4.1.21)

Unlike some other schools, the Nyaya did not take the existence of God as a given and in their typical rigorous style, they felt the need to defend the idea from rival schools (such as the Buddhists) and to build it into their ontological framework.

They developed a number of arguments for the existence of God, many resembling arguments which were used much later by European philosophy in the middle ages and onwards.

The First Cause Argument

Entities cannot be said to be produced from no-cause, because the no-cause is, according to some, the cause of the production.
(Nyaya Sutra, 4.1.23)

They made use of the 'first cause' argument which says that if all things have a cause, then so must the universe. They believe there must be a 'first cause', which itself is 'uncaused', otherwise tracing causes back would continue infinitely, which is unsatisfactory to them (remember their reluctance to accept infinite division, so too with infinite regression). So as there must be a first cause, the Nyaya argue that this must be God.

A Popular counter argument to this is that it denies the possibility of something being eternal, and that it is not necessarily illogical to posit that the universe is eternal.

The Nyaya respond by saying that they are not denying eternalness as a possible concept, however as the physical universe can be perceived and proven to be subject to creation and destruction, then it cannot be eternal, as eternal things cannot be created or destroyed. The Nyaya do accept the existence of some eternal things, like the soul, or God, however they still believe God is the cause of the physical, non eternal Universe:

> ***There is no denial of the eternal, as there is a regulation as to the character of our perception.***
> ***(Nyaya Sutra, 4.1.28)***

> ***Whatever is perceived to be produced or destroyed is non-eternal and that which is not so is eternal, e. g., there is no perceptual evidence as to the production or destruction of ether, time, space, soul, mind, generality, particularity and intimate relation.***
> ***Consequently these are eternal.***
> ***(Nyaya Sutra, 4.1.28)***

Self or Soul

For the Nyaya, liberation (Moksha) from the realm of existence would involve 'realising' the true nature of the soul, through correct knowledge and shedding ignorance, and thus liberating the soul from the physical realm. Other Hindu schools put more of an emphasis on ethics, or physical practises as their means of liberation.

The Nyaya had a concept of mind, which they called 'Manas'. They believed that the mind played the role of synthesising together the various perceptions of the body into feelings and consciousness. The mind was thought to be subject to creation and destruction and thus impermanent.

So in this context, when we say 'self' we are referring to the Atman (higher self) mixed with the Manas (mind) in any one given lifetime. However the Nyaya argued this was temporary, and the soul would leave the mind upon death, and move on to another. They argued that it was false knowledge that led you to identify with your mind as your true self.

They believed that whilst a soul was on earth, it was intricately linked to a mind and formed a combination unique to each lifetime. It is the soul though, which is perceived to be the enduring substance which migrates between lifetimes.

The arguments for the existence of an enduring soul were often met with dispute from the Buddhists, who as a heterodox school did not believe in the existence of an everlasting self or soul (as discussed in the previous chapter)

Nyaya argued that memories, thoughts and perceptions form a synthesis together which makes up consciousness, but consciousness itself cannot exist on its own. They thought that consciousness must have a subject to which it 'belongs' and this is what they called the Atman.

Atman, body, senses, objects of senses, intellect, mind, activity, error, pretyabhava (after life), fruit, suffering and bliss are the objects of right knowledge. Desire, aversion, effort, happiness, suffering and cognition are the Linga of the Atman.
(Nyaya Sutra, 1.1.9-10)

For the Nyaya, the concept of Atman was crucial in explaining how Karma could be carried between lifetimes. They argued that Karma was intricately linked to the Atman, who then carried it between different physical bodies and lives.

Time:

The Nyaya defended the concept of time as being real. Again, this may seem a common sense position, but it was important for them to defend these bedrocks of knowledge against sceptics. After all, it is difficult to justify knowledge of the past without a belief in time.

Some other schools denied time as having any reality, and instead saw it as a useful tool, or just a subjective perception which didn't really exist. The Nyaya argued that time was a necessary concept for knowledge, as memory, testimony and inference rely on there being a coherent past.

The past and the future cannot be established by mere mutual reference... If there was no present time, sense perception would be impossible, knowledge would be impossible.
(Nyaya Sutra, 2.1.41)

Note how the Nyaya tend to look for areas which could lead to scepticism about knowledge and do their best to defend the concepts (such as time, testimony, inference) which support their epistemology. This is because they rely on their epistemological framework to justify their version of how one can reach liberation from the cycle of death and rebirth.

Summary

- Nyaya is an orthodox school of Hindu philosophy which defends core orthodox principles such as Brahman, Karma, Atman and Samsara through argument and logic, and shares a metaphysical framework with the Vaisesika school.
- Nyaya is a realist school, arguing for the direct existence of a material universe, which exists independently of human perception.
- Nyaya argues that the key to salvation from the eternal rounds of reincarnation is the correct knowledge.
- Therefore epistemology is particularly important to the Nyaya, who were early pioneers in discussing the problems of induction, testimony and perception.
- Whilst not as widely studied outside of India now as Yoga or Buddhism, Nyaya is crucial to the development of Indian philosophy due to the rigorous defence and argument for orthodox positions.

Chapter 5:

INTRODUCTION TO CHINESE PHILOSOPHY

China is a vast nation, with a unique history and mix of cultures dating back thousands of years. Chinese civilisation is one of the oldest still in existence, with evidence of court records dating back to the 8th century BC, and poetry and musical texts dating back to between 10th-8th century BC. Further back still there is evidence of writing being used as early as 1200-1000 BC.

As ever there are debates about exact dating, but what cannot be in doubt is that we are dealing with an ancient society with a tradition of writing and civilisation that dates back at least three thousand years. With this in mind, we can discuss some fundamentals of the two most influential schools of philosophy to originate in China: Taoism and Confucianism.

Over the millennia, Chinese society has largely been an agricultural and feudal one, with the vast majority of the population engaged in either farming, letting and leasing farmland, or serving that industry. Chinese history is rife with various states, rulers and clans warring, merging, and splitting apart.

However despite the fractious nature of the political climate, there is a distinct Chinese character and culture which was formed and maintained, and this is in no small part due to the work of the prominent philosophers, who alongside religion, art, literature, and politics, determined much of the modern Chinese society and character.

Confucius (551-479 BC) is probably the best known and most influential Chinese philosopher. His teachings had immense influence and are amongst the earliest surviving written systems of ideas from China.

Lao Tzu, who authored the *Tao Te Ching* and is the father of Taoism is said to have lived between the 6th and 4th century BC.

Both of these figures lived and wrote in the era which is known as the period of 'a hundred schools' in which many systems of philosophy developed and engaged with one another, and came to define Chinese society- such as Confucianism, Taoism, Legalism, and Mohism.

Within the multitude of influential philosophers, there are often said to be three main 'Jewels' or systems of ideas which have defined Chinese culture. These are Confucianism, Taoism, and Buddhism. Buddhism was translated into Chinese in roughly the 5th century AD, and came to be adopted and has vast influence in China to this day. In many ways it absorbed and evolved many of the cultural traditions of China, as is common with external religions. The Unique character of Chinese Buddhism still does rely on the issues discussed in the second chapter as a foundation.

A common theme of Chinese philosophy is what may be described in modern terms as Humanism. Whilst Confucianism and Taoism both deal with mystical, and quasi religious themes, the core focus is with a humans' relationship to life. In the Confucian sense this is more directed toward society and family, and in the Taoist sense towards nature and the inner self. Nevertheless there is a shared focus on personal improvement, and a clear lack of appeal to God or supernatural forces to justify these systems of thought.

Another common theme is a focus on political leadership, and the cohesiveness of society in general. Both Confucianism and Taoism discuss the nature of leadership in relation to the family and wider society. Confucianism in particular focuses on society, proper relations between people and family unity as foundations. Both Confucianism and Taoism discuss family relations and politics, which is more a reflection of Chinese tradition at the time than new developments of their own, however this focus has carried these themes through to modern Chinese society.

Tian is a central concept to Chinese mythology and philosophy, translated roughly as heaven, or sky. Tian is regarded as the supreme spiritual reality of life, represented by the stars or the sky. It is not a creator God figure or a deity so much as a guide and a force. The concept of Tian is seen as the moral ordering of things, via a natural metaphor. It is very much tied up with fate and morality, and with the idea that life has an order. However it is not at all fatalist in the sense that human behaviour is predestined. In fact it is the humanism of Chinese philosophy which views the human task to coordinate their behaviour so as to work with Tian, and they must have free will to do so.

Confucius regarded Tian as a force of good which could guide the action of men.

Another common thread in Chinese philosophy is a focus on names. Whether it be the proper terminology for legal terms, or a focus on social structures and their relationships or more metaphysical and natural concerns. The use of the Chinese language differs from Romanised and Western alphabets as it is not a phonetic language (meaning words are spelled out via letters). Rather it is a system of writing in which each character may have a multitude of meanings associated with it, therefore debate and focus on what a particular word means became a focus of Chinese philosophy. This makes translation particularly difficult, and always subject to interpretation (even more so than with the Sanskrit texts)

One example of prominent focus on a name as a theme is with the word *Tao*. Tao can be very roughly translated to 'way' or 'path' and refers to a style or mode of being or living. Whilst Taoism has become defined by one particular interpretation of Tao, the term itself is used throughout Chinese philosophy in many contexts.

As with the Indian schools, Chinese philosophy is greatly influenced by native traditional systems of thought such as astrology, medicine, politics, arts, and physical pursuits. It is beyond the scope of this book to examine how one has influenced the other, however it should be noted that here the focus is on the systems of ideas which are laid forth and can stand in their own right.

Confucianism and Taoism have been selected for focus, largely due to their immense influence on Chinese and far east Asian culture and society. They represent two quite different strands of Chinese philosophy that nevertheless overlap in many themes and focuses.

Chapter 6:

TAOISM

***There was something formless and perfect before the universe was born...
For lack of a better name, I call it the Tao.
(Tao Te Ching, 1)***

Taoism is both a spiritual tradition and a philosophy, traced back to *Lao Tzu*. Lao Tzu is an honorary name, meaning 'ancient sage or master' and his given name was said to be 'Li'. There is debate around when he lived, he is often said to be a contemporary of Confucius (6th Century BC), although this ranges towards the 4th Century BC. Taoism is characterised by a subtle, mystical approach to life and is inspired by the constant change and interdependent opposites of nature.

The central text of Taoism is the '*Tao Te Ching*', ('The Book of the Way'). It is a collection of sayings, written in a mystical and poetic style. Lao Tzu is traditionally thought of as the author. There is debate as to whether this was all written by Lao Tzu, or is a composite of many authors over the following centuries. There is even legitimate debate as to whether Lao Tzu existed, or is just a mythical figure. Either way, the book was written, and has had such a profound impact on the Eastern world, that it has come to define its own religion and philosophy which is considered to be one of the two major native philosophies of China (along with Confucianism).

The Secondary text of Daoism is the *Zhuangzi*, written by the author of the same name who is a philosopher said to have lived in the 4th Century BC, and to have been a follower of Lao Tzu. This text is more like a literary work, and contains stories, fables and parables which are often humorous, portraying the life of an ideal 'Sage' who lives in the Taoist way.

Taoism is often also Romanised (written in the Western alphabet) as 'Daoism', using a D instead of a T. Likewise the T*ao Te Ching* can be Romanised as '*Dao De Ching*'. They mean the same thing. The actual pronunciation in Chinese sounds more like a D than a T. However for many years now the use of a T has been popularised, so is used here in accordance with that.

Taoism is a mixture of many schools of thought and traditions which pre-date Lao Tzu and Zhuangzi, and were developed after them. Some scholars trace the roots of Taoism to hermits and sages who are mentioned in various other texts (such as the *Analects* of Confucianism). Here we will focus on what may be called the philosophy of Taoism, and the traditional view that Lao Tzu authored the primary text, the *Tao Te Ching*, and refer mainly to that, with also some reference to the *Zhuangzi.*

The religious aspect of Taoism is the applied philosophy, mixed with beliefs (many cultural, preceding Taoism) about the nature of the universe, including aspects of astrology, medicine and cosmology. The spiritual practice of Taoism may be said to be the application of the ideas which are supported by the key texts.

Whilst it is difficult to completely separate philosophy from the spiritual side (as they ultimately are from the same source), here we will focus on Taoism as a philosophy, and a set of ideas about life, nature and the universe.

Taoism is a mystical path, shrouded in myth and legend. However, there is a clear and consistent approach to life portrayed in the *Tao De Ching* and the *Zhuangzhi,* which taken together form a distinct outlook.

The word 'Tao' is central to ancient and modern Chinese thought, and is not actually unique to Taoism. The word is roughly translated to 'Way'. Way is an apt translation as it is broad enough to cover the many meanings of 'Tao', whilst also acknowledging that there can be many 'ways'. Other translations are *path* or *road.* The sense that Tao encapsulates the idea of a route or certain journey is clear.

The Tao

Explaining the Tao is a difficult task. It is a mysterious concept at best. It is no coincidence that the first two lines of the *Tao Te Ching* warn us against trying to name or define it:

> ***The tao that can be told is not the eternal Tao The name that can be named is not the eternal Name.***
> ***(Tao Te Ching, 1)***

It is not clear that the Tao is something you can really 'know', moreover it is something you can live or experience.

Tao is often described as 'flowing through all things'. It is a subtle concept that cannot be intellectually grasped. Lao Tzu is keen to emphasise that the Tao is a lived philosophy:

> ***My teachings are easy to understand***
> ***and easy to put into practice.***
> ***Yet your intellect will never grasp them...***
> ***(Tao Te Ching, 70)***

The Tao is not exactly a God (or 'god'). However, it is said to support and precede the universe, which are two qualities often associated with divine beings. It may be thought of as a fundamental 'energy' or 'force' that is inherent in all things, is the cause of all things and cannot be defined by itself.

Since before time and space were, the Tao is.
It is beyond is and is not.
(Tao Te Ching, 21)

In the beginning was the Tao.
All things issue from it; all things return to it.
(Tao Te Ching, 25)

In order to feel the Tao, It helps to first have an understanding of some of the key themes of the *Tao Te Ching.*

The *Tao Te Ching* reads a bit like a book of poetry. The wording is such that you could read one verse many times, and each time understand it in a different context. It refers largely to universal principles, and has a particular focus on nature, impermanence, opposites, and how best to live.

Of all philosophies discussed in this book, Taoism is perhaps the one which requires the most use of the primary text, as the meaning of the Tao is to be drawn from each passage, rather than just explained through logic or reason.

Desire

Free from desire, you realise the mystery.
Caught in desire, you see only the manifestations.
(Tao Te Ching, 1)

As with Buddhism, aversion to desire is a central concept in Taoist thought. Desire is understood to be a mental state that is incompatible with peace and balance:

When there is no desire, all things are at peace.
(Tao Te Ching, 37)

To grasp the mystery of the Tao, one first must be free from the desire to seek it. But this is a sort of paradox; how can somebody understand something without the desire to do so?

It is not as illogical as it seems. For example, take the process of unconsciously learning a skill. A young child may learn how to ride a bike one day without ever having knowledge or desire of bikes, but is put on one by his father and shown the way, thus gaining an understanding. In the same way, one can realise the Tao only without desiring to do so.

Be content with what you have; rejoice in the way things are. When you realise there is nothing lacking, the whole world belongs to you.
(Tao Te Ching, 44)

Lao Tzu taught that living in a constant state of desire and yearning for the future, or for external things, is the antithesis of living with the Tao. Therefore one had to let go of desire and be at ease with the way things are to live in the best way.

Wu Wei

> ***Acting with no expectations, leading and not trying to control: this is the supreme virtue. (Tao Te Ching, 10)***

Wu Wei can be roughly translated as 'effortless action', or 'non-doing'. The idea is that an action is best performed in a state of 'flow' in which there is no mental desire to reach an outcome, rather there is a focus on being absorbed in the task itself.

For example, a farmer may plant seeds and eagerly water and watch them, with a firm idea in his mind of the need to produce his desired goal: the crop. This desire, under a Taoist understanding (although perhaps rational) removes him from 'the Way'.

To perform this action with 'Wu Wei', one would plant the seeds, and nurture them, with no thought of the end product, just to be with them in each stage of their growth. The outcome will be the same, as the necessary action of tending the seeds is still performed. But when done with 'Wu Wei' the act of farming becomes less stressful. In fact, under this way of thinking, the farmer is more likely to tend the seed better, as he will be more focused on the present moment and noticing the seeds and surrounding conditions themselves, rather than an imagined end goal.

Why waste further energy, on the mental focus of the outcome of an action, rather than be totally with the action at hand? Wu Wei, does not mean 'no action'. That would lead to stagnation, and would not be in accordance with nature. It means to act in the moment, free of desire.

Wu Wei, also means to act without a sense of self, as the desire for an outcome is often ultimately rooted in a sense of ego, and how the outcome will benefit or harm ones' self. To properly practice Wu Wei, Lao Tzu states we must act without self, and be part of the process of nature rather than an observer trying to 'manipulate' it.

He lets all things come and go effortlessly, without desire. He never expects results; thus he is never disappointed.
(Tao Te Ching, 55)

The Master takes action by letting things take their course. He remains as calm at the end as at the beginning. He has nothing, thus has nothing to lose. What he desires is non-desire.
(Tao Te Ching, 63)

As with most other concepts in the *Tao Te Ching*, Wu Wei is centred in the rhythms of nature. The concept is understood as a subtle and gentle way of activity, which leads to work with less friction, stress or anxiety.

The gentlest thing in the world overcomes the hardest thing in the world. That which has no substance enters where there is no space. This shows the value of non-action.
(Tao Te Ching, 43)

Wu Wei may initially seem a contradiction in terms. It has been the subject of hundreds of years of debate between different Chinese, and later Western scholars. Ultimately though, it means to become absorbed in action, and focus on that rather than straining or fretting about the outcome. As with many other Taoist concepts, it is something to be experienced rather than just intellectually grasped.

Opposites

> ***Being and non-being create each other.***
> ***Difficult and easy support each other.***
> ***Long and short define each other.***
> ***High and low depend on each other.***
> ***Before and after follow each other.***
> ***(Tao Te Ching, 2)***

The *Tao Te Ching* places an emphasis on opposite qualities which rely on each other to become a 'whole'. This theme may be expressed as 'Unity of Opposites', and has a few functions in Taoist philosophy.

It can be understood as a holistic view, meaning the Taoist takes into account the totality of all things, rather than their separate parts, and understands that one thing (e.g. a tall mountain) is defined by another, (e.g. flat land). In this sense the *Tao Te Ching* reminds us that opposites complement one another. For a mountain cannot be said to be tall if there is nothing small or flat that it is taller than.

This view has a few functions. Psychologically it can give us a sense of balance, to remember that mental states and emotions are dependent on their opposite, and that we can transcend a 'normal' view of the world (seeing a room full of separate objects) to a view more in line with the Tao (seeing a room of interdependent objects, reliant on each other, forming a whole unity).

The concept of 'Yin and yang' is famously associated with Taoism (although it predates it), and represents both the masculine and feminine, or light and dark in all things. Masculine and feminine is not meant to literally mean biology, rather the different 'energies' pervasive in the universe. One person can partake in both of these energies. Yin represents the more passive 'feminine' energy, and Yang the active 'masculine' energy.

The opposites described here such as hard and soft, tall and short, high and low, are understood to be part of the ultimate 'oneness' or Tao, only which can transcend the boundaries of the particular things in the universe. Opposites support each other, so are part of the same whole.

All things are born of being.
Being is born of non-being.
(Tao Te Ching, 40)

Non-Being is another fundamental concept. Lao Tzu argued that everything in the universe originates from a void of 'non being', and relies on 'non being' for purpose.

For example, a doorway was created from nothing (non being) by action. It is the empty space (non being) inside the frame (being) which makes it useful. Therefore, being and non being compliment each other as opposites. The principle here is that the existence of anything relies on the existence of a void, from which it came, and which it exists 'in' or 'around'. There cannot be 'something' without a 'nothing' for it to contrast with.

***We work with being,
but non-being is what we use.
(Tao Te Ching, 11)***

***He who wants to have right without wrong,
Order without disorder, Does not
understand the principles of heaven and earth.
(Chang Tzu, 17)***

Nature

***Be like the forces of nature:
when it blows, there is only wind;
when it rains, there is only rain;
when the clouds pass, the sun shines through.
If you open yourself to the Tao,
you are at one with the Tao.
(Tao Te Ching, 43)***

Taoism is based on observations of nature. If the Tao can be said to 'be' anything (which we know it cannot) it would be nature, or at least nature would be the embodiment of it. The *Tao Te Ching* is full of reference to nature, and to the natural balance of the world. This is based on the understanding that nature has a rhythm and intelligence which people should follow.

The Tao Te Ching regularly recommends that in life one should do what needs doing, and then rest. This is based on the observation that nature has phases and then rests, e.g. a rainstorm which then ceases, or a baking hot day which cools in the evening.

The *Tao Te Ching* reflects the constant flux and change of the natural world and advises us to work within these changes and not resist them. Clinging to a solid concept of life is in itself a form of desire which is not the way of the Taoist sage.

Lao Tzu believed that nature is self regulating, and has a natural intelligence, which is beyond the comprehension of humans to understand or manipulate. He warned against trying to tamper with nature and instead, advised us to work within its rhythms. It is very much a 'hands off' philosophy.

Do you want to improve the world?
I don't think it can be done. The world is sacred.
It can't be improved.
If you tamper with it, you'll ruin it.
If you treat it like an object, you'll lose it.
(Tao Te Ching, 29)

Lao Tzu compared the ancient Sages to the qualities of nature, further demonstrating how deeply this philosophy is rooted in natural observations:

The Ancient Masters were... Fluid as melting ice. Shapeable as a block of wood. Receptive as a valley. Clear as a glass of water.
(Tao Te Ching, 15)

Lao Tzu particularly revered the ability of the natural world to change, be non fixed, and work within a unity of opposites. He rejected fixed absolute notions of what a person or sage should be. He rather leant towards venerating qualities of the universe itself and trying to embody them.

Colours blind the eye. Sounds deafen the ear. Flavours numb the taste.
(Tao Te Ching, 12)

This verse is typical of the paradoxical style of Taoism. One interpretation of this verse is that Lao Tzu seems to suggest that potentiality, and having a direct connection with our perception of nature is important.

The names of things (such as our senses) are useful tools, but are also rooted in society, and give us a mental scheme which breaks the direct connection between us and nature. If we sit and gaze at a waterfall, and focus on the name of each colour we see or sound we hear all as separate phenomena, we lose our direct connection. Lao Tzu alludes to a master seeing things as holistic:

The Master observes the world but trusts his inner vision. He allows things to come and go.
(Tao Te Ching, 12)

Ultimately, the Tao is described as the force which precedes and directs nature, and causes it to act so economically:

It adjusts excess and deficiency so that there is perfect balance. It takes from what is too much and gives to what isn't enough.
(Tao Te Ching, 77)

Politics

Act for the people's benefit. Trust them; leave them alone.
(Tao Te Ching, 74)

Taoism offers a *laissez-faire* attitude to government and politics, advising rulers to avoid domination, control or too much intervention into the lives of the citizens. Instead, Lao Tzu advised 'ruling without clinging'. Taoism in this sense, differs from the other dominant philosophies of the era in which it evolved (Confucianism, Legalism), and was heavily criticised for this.

Taoism is often interpreted in a political sense as anti-authoritarian, and has been regarded as some as an ancient pretext to anarchism.

There is no assigned set of social principles that all people should follow (unlike Confucianism). Instead it is a pluralist philosophy, meaning it accepts a multitude of 'truths' or ways of living that people could follow. As discussed, general principles of peace, softness, and living in rhythm with nature are encouraged. However, there are little prescribed social roles, or particular rituals or customs which are dictated down to followers. Many rituals have become associated with the spiritual side of Taoism, but dogma is mostly avoided.

As with other influential Chinese philosophies of the time (such as Confucianism and Legalism) Taoism is rife with reference to leadership and politics, with a focus on the collective. In typical style of the *Tao Te Ching* the references are not direct orders to a certain type of political leadership, nor does it address any technical issues for a government to follow (although it does advise against over taxing citizens). The advice is intentionally vague and poetic.

Instead it is a philosophy of leadership or ruling that can be applied to any area of life and is rooted in the paradox that the more you try to dominate or control something, the harder it will be and you will eventually lose it. Instead Lao Tzu asserts that being a ruler is subtle art, which involves care and attention, from a place of detachment. The philosophy on leadership can perhaps best be summarised by the verse:

All streams flow to the sea because it is lower than they are. Humility gives it its power.
(Tao Te Ching, 66)

The idea here is paradoxical and again an example of unity of opposites, and an instruction based in observation of nature. The Ruler is asked to behave like the sea, 'below' his subjects, letting the power flow into him, by receiving, rather than trying to dominate them. The verse continues to mention this directly:

If you want to govern the people, you must place yourself below them. If you want to lead the people, you must learn how to follow them.
(Tao Te Ching, 66)

Those who try to control, who use force to protect their power, go against the direction of the Tao.
(Tao Te Ching, 77)

The *Tao Te Ching* certainly seems opposed to authoritarian rule, and overt control of people. Instead leaning towards a respect for the will of people, and advising rulers to intervene as little as possible, whilst arranging the affairs of a nation quietly.

Above all when it comes to leadership in all forms, whether that be of a family, a state, or a business, Lao Tzu advises us to mimic the Tao, by not dominating, and instead 'feeding'. This is clearly a very important point to Lao Tzu, as it is listed as the final words of the *Tao Te Ching*:

> ***The Tao nourishes by not forcing.***
> ***By not dominating, the Master leads.***
> ***(Tao Te Ching, 81)***

Peace and Compassion

Themes of softness, peace, and compassion for others are key to Taoism. The humanism of self improvement is intended as a tool to be extended outwards towards helping others.

> ***...whoever is stiff and inflexible is a disciple of death. Whoever is soft and yielding is a disciple of life....The hard and stiff will be broken.***
> ***The soft and supple will prevail.***
> ***(Tao Te Ching, 76)***

This is another example of a lesson from the observable world being applied to human life. Lao Tzu asserted that being 'hard' or inflexible is not a strength, and will lead to one being unable to handle the hardships and pain of life. Being soft is a strength as to be soft is to be adaptable and supple.

The soft overcomes the hard; the gentle overcomes the rigid....Therefore the Master remains serene in the midst of sorrow.... he has given up helping, he is people's greatest help... True words seem paradoxical.
(Tao Te Ching, 78)

Passage 31 in the *Tao Te Ching* refers to violence as a last resort and says that one attending a battle should do so sadly, as though they were at a funeral. This tells us that Taoism is not totally pacifist and acknowledges violence may be necessary, but should never be desired. Peace is referred to as the 'highest value'.

Weapons are the tools of violence; all decent men detest them....a decent man will avoid them except in the direst necessity .... Peace is his highest value...How could he rejoice in victory and delight in the slaughter of men?
(Tao Te Ching, 31)

The recognition of the inter-relation between all things serves as a further reason for not harming others, as there is a self in others and others in self. Taoism recognises peace as a virtue in society, cultivated through the behaviours and thoughts of each individual. Therefore, the focus is primarily on how to achieve peace within a person, through the right approach to life, rather than directions on the proper relations between people or government. The onus is on an individual to first cultivate their inner world and then affect the outer world.

Cosmology: Microcosm and Macrocosm

Taoists conceive of the universe as an expression of the Tao. In this sense, all things in the universe are manifestations of the same source and therefore operate with similar principles or patterns. Taoists believe then that the same patterns are at play in a human cell (microcosm) as they are in a star system (macrocosm). Under this conception of the universe, all things affect each other and are interrelated, as everything is a manifestation of one source.

This idea came to greatly influence Chinese culture, medicine, astrology and society. This is in keeping with the view of traditional Chinese medicine that the human body is an internal universe which reflects the external.

Taoism has had a great influence on the development of traditional Chinese medicine. For example, The concept of unity of opposites, has influenced the theory of there being feminine and masculine energies within the body.

Taoism is also closely related to Qi Gong, which is a meditation practice based on the idea of balancing energies in the body via the meridian channels. The meridian channels are understood as pathways of bio electricity or 'Qi' in the body.

Names

The *Tao Te Ching* encourages us (when possible) to return our minds to a primal state of being 'unformed'. When we name things, we form concepts in our minds and discriminate between things. The names are largely given to us by society, and cause us to be 'socialised' and desire or reject certain things which are prized by our culture. This is of course useful and has a function to help us navigate the world, however Lao Tzu believed it was better to dwell in a more primordial state of mind, which was free from discrimination between things, and saw the world as one unity. Hence the focus on Names is important to Taoism.

Lao Tzu advised 'forgetting names' as a practice of freeing our minds, and allowing us to live in a simpler, more spontaneous way.

When you have names and forms, know that they are provisional. ...Knowing when to stop, you can avoid any danger. (Tao Te Ching, 32)

There is an acknowledgment that naming things can cause fixed ideas in our minds which can lead to rigid, unchanging thinking, which is inconsistent with the Tao. Lao Tzu reminds us that names are themselves impermanent and whilst they serve a use, we should not be beholden to them.

This is emphasised by the fact that Tao itself, cannot be formally named- as it is eternal and primordial. Therefore, we can understand that things which are named are temporary.

The name that can be named is not the eternal Name. The unnameable is the eternally real. Naming is the origin of all particular things. (Tao Te Ching, 1)

Relativism

The whole universe is treated as one ultimate reality, which is 'nourished' by the Tao. The difference between things (e.g. a mountain being large in comparison to a mouse) is understood as only a relative difference. A mountain cannot be said to be 'large' in any objective sense, only in relation to other things, as it would be small in comparison to a planet.

This relativism is also applied to moral concepts such as 'good' and 'bad' (Which are understood to only be comparisons between things). This type of relativism is mentioned in the *Chuang Tzu*

> ***When we look at things in the light of Tao, Nothing is best, nothing is worst.... What is smaller than something else is "small," Therefore there is nothing that is not "small." So the whole cosmos is a grain of rice, and the tip of a hair is as big as a mountain...Such is the relative view.***
> ***(Chang Tzu, 12)***

Chang Tzu notes the principle of 'similarity-difference', recognising that all things have differences and similarities, no matter which two things you choose or how initially different they may seem. This form of relativism is not intended to deny that there are differences between things, rather to highlight that properties (whether moral, or physical) exist only in relation to each other. This view sits neatly with the holism of Taoism, and the 'unity of opposites'- Chang Tzu reminds us that.

Ethics

Taoism does not set out a specific agenda of moral rules such as the ten commandments, nor does it tend toward mentioning specific areas of life which should be focused on for the good of society like Confucianism. Instead we can gather from the *Tao Te Ching* that ethics of Taoism are generally speaking: non-violence, harmony with nature, transcendence of material desire, respect of others freedom and as much as possible non-interference with the way things are.

Sages

Taoist sages exist to this day, and are usually hermits who retreat from society and practice rituals in seclusion. They aim to live with the patterns of nature, free from desire and distraction of the modern world, and be at one with the Tao.

Conclusion

Taoism is a subtle, mystical philosophy rooted in observations of nature, and encourages a calm temperament. It avoids the detailed logical and epistemological debates of Indian and Western schools, and instead focuses on a root concept (the Tao) with which to analyse all things through. It has had a vast impact on the far East and is accepted as one of the two main philosophies of China. Ultimately it is a system rooted in more ancient ideas, and based in practice, and its utility is how it can be applied to a human life to improve well-being and live in flow with nature.

There is no definite way to define Taoism, it isn't a system, it is not quite a religion. We can say for sure, the *Tao Te Ching* is a teaching for anyone who will listen. Whilst Taoism is a philosophy that resists rigid definition, perhaps we can simplify it by looking at verse 67. Lao Tzu distilled his philosophy into three simple treasures:

> ***I have just three things to teach: simplicity, patience, compassion.***
> ***These three are your greatest treasures.***
> ***(Tao Te Ching, 67)***

Chapter 7:

CONFUCIANISM

Confucius was a philosopher, teacher and political scholar who lived between 551–479 BC in what is now modern day China. He is regarded as being one of the most influential philosophers of all time due to the vast influence his work had in the subsequent millennia in China, surrounding east Asian countries, and later the West. His teachings have been so influential that they are largely considered ubiquitous with Chinese culture.

Confucius' work is largely secular without direct appeal to a God or religion for moral authority (although veneration of ancestors is a key theme). He was mainly concerned with virtuous behaviour, social cohesion, family values, political leadership, ritual and the arts. His teachings are based on the idea that everyone has a role to play in society, and that social customs are the glue which holds civilisation together.

The enormous impact his work has had on China and surrounding countries could be compared to the impact of the Bible in other parts of the world. It can be fairly said that one needs an understanding of Confucian principles if one wants to understand Chinese culture and social customs. There is no doubt that he is one of the most influential philosophers of all time.

His teachings are presented in texts that have become known as the 'Five classics', and perhaps the most fundamental of these is *The Analects,* a book of Confucian sayings.

Confucius was born into a well regarded family, in what is now eastern China (Shandong province) though raised in poverty after his father died when he was only three years old. He lived in a time of war and political instability, which surely moulded his world view. He took up governmental administration jobs in his twenties, before leaving his province to travel and spread his teachings, enduring many hardships along the way. He finally returned to his homeland, and took up political office and began teaching to his disciples. It is these teachings which are distilled in *The Analects.*

Confucius was concerned about the divided nature of his homeland and saw his teachings as an attempt to repopularise a previous, more united era of rule. He was frustrated by poor political leadership and a lack of proper moral conduct in his society. He believed a leader should be steeped in moral philosophy, and act within traditional social customs and therefore be respected rather than feared by his subjects. He envisaged a benevolent king, a ruler who had a deep moral imperative, who the people could respect, model their behaviour on, and serve in the proper fashion. He saw this as the mandate of heaven.

The role of family was central to Confucius' teachings and he believed that the concept of 'filial piety' (respecting and caring for your elder family members) was fundamental to a decent society and the model on which proper behaviour of a citizen could be built. The family unit served as a building block to the function of society for Confucius. Veneration of ancestors in carefully ordered rituals was an important part of this process. The values can be said to be conservative in many ways, with a preference toward family, tradition, and respect for elders.

Above all, Confucius' philosophy was an ethical one which placed emphasis on the individual to act as a 'Sage' or 'Gentleman', to reject their base instincts and instead act in a manner which is best for themselves, and by turn society.

Ethical self development, cultivation of skills, the arts and serving family and society were all encouraged. There is an implicit suggestion of free will, and personal responsibility.

As with many ancient philosophers, Confucius' writings and works are shrouded in debate and conjecture as to who exactly wrote which part, at what time. There are however clear consistent threads of teachings throughout his main works, and it is likely his disciples recorded much of his teachings (as with the Buddha and Jesus).

Confucius' teachings may be categorised into three broad areas:

- **Society & humanity**
- **Virtues**
- **Ritual**

There are many works attributed to Confucius and his teachings. This chapter will rely largely on *The Four Books*, which are introductions and fundamentals to Confucian philosophy. These books contain:

The Analects – A compilation of sayings and teachings from Confucius and his disciples, covering most aspects of his philosophy, particularly his ethical teachings.

The Book of Rites- (containing the *Great Learning* and the *Doctrine of the Mean*) This is a textbook of ancient rituals and ceremonies and how they should be properly performed and the ethical context behind them.

Mencius- A collection of sayings, conversations and teachings by one of the most influential Confucian scholars, Mencius.

Ethics

The Gentleman [Junzi] gets through to what is up above; the small man gets through to what is down below.
(Analects, 14:23)

Confucian' ethics are arguably a version of 'virtue ethics'. Virtue ethics is a way of dealing with moral philosophy. Rather than focusing on the outcome of an action, or 'rules' set by a leader or a 'God' figure, virtue ethics focus on the conduct and character of the individual performing an action. The idea is that a certain behaviour or attitude is seen as virtuous, rather than a specific outcome. It is a type of ethics that assumes free will, and responsibility of the agent.

Confucius recognised that the virtues he encouraged are not absolute and are difficult to embody. However he makes it clear they constitute a superior model of behaviour from which both the agent and the whole society benefits and they are a goal to aim for.

Take the phrase: 'do not steal'. From a Christian perspective, this would be dictated by God. From an outcome based perspective, this would be argued for by demonstrating that stealing has negative consequences on other people, or on yourself. However from a virtue ethics perspective the focus would be on the behaviour or moral character of the person. It would argue that one should not steal as this is not the 'virtuous' or benevolent way to act and that society benefits most when people act in a virtuous way.

Confucius projected the idea of an ideal person, (a *Junzi)* in his writings. This is often translated as a 'sage' or 'gentleman', although is not a gender specific term, as both male and female contribute to this role.

Confucius described and advocated for a number of virtues or proper behaviours, which he believed were the components of a 'sage' or 'gentleman'. Rather than having a spiritual or metaphysical 'end goal', like in many other traditions, Confucius' aims appear to be mostly secular. He was concerned with a cohesive and functioning society, in which all members played their proper role.

Confucius indicated that his vision of ethics was not lofty, or far from the mind of the everyday person, and that it was, in a sense, innate in all of us to know what is right:

> ***The Master said "The path is not far from man. When men try to pursue a course, which is far from the common indications of consciousness, this course cannot be considered The Path". (The Doctorine of the Mean, 13:1)***

Perhaps the most complete and comprehensive of the virtues is Confucius' own version of the 'golden rule'. This is a rule which appears in various forms in moral and religious texts amongst many different cultures throughout history.

The Golden Rule (Known as 'Shu')

> ***Is there a word which can be a guide to conduct throughout one's life? The Master said, 'It is perhaps the word "shu". Do not impose on others what you yourself do not desire.***
> ***(Analects, 15:24)***

The Confucian version of this rule is phrased as a negative, 'do not impose on others' rather than a positive 'do to others'... This rule can be seen as an overarching principle for his moral philosophy and points to his concern for the well-being of the group rather than any one individual.

The Five Virtues:

- **Benevolence ('Ren')**

An attitude, grounded in compassion and consideration for others over oneself. Known as 'Ren' in Chinese this is considered an attitude that combines the Confucian virtues and exemplifies them via outward expression of love, respect or compassion for others.

> ***Fan Ch'ih asked about benevolence.***
> ***The Master said, "Love your fellow men".***
> ***(Analects, 12:22)***

Confucius took this virtue very seriously, and even considered it to be a principle of life and death.

> ***For Gentlemen of purpose ... it may happen that they have to accept death in***

order to have benevolence accomplished.
(Analects, 15:9)

Benevolence may be considered the 'supreme' Confucian virtue and is ultimately an attitude of acting with total consideration of others. It is the polar opposite of selfishness, individualism and greed. It exemplifies the social, person centred nature of Confucian' ethics, and is deeply ingrained in the communal attitude of Chinese society to this day.

- **Righteousness**

Righteousness was regarded by Confucius as a choice when faced with temptation or the option of corruption, often in the context of government or family. For example if one has an opportunity to steal some money when nobody's looking, and they know they would not be caught. The righteous thing would be to resist the temptation regardless of being seen or not, as this is a virtue.

If a man remembers what is right at the sight of profit... he may be said to be a complete man.
(Analects, 14:12)

Righteousness is rooted in consideration of others and the societal impact of any action. Confucius is considered to have been so righteous, as he served his society properly in his role working in courts, whilst not seeking further profit or gain despite his lack of material wealth.

This is not to say that having money or material wealth was demonised by Confucius, as it is recognised that there are rulers, and social ranks. It is to say that money should not be the primary consideration for action. Righteousness as a principle works both ways, as a ruler is expected to be righteous when taking decisions about society, as a subject should be righteous toward their ruler.

- **Ritual Propriety**

Confucius believed that ritual was a cornerstone of a healthy and cohesive society and therefore one of the most important moral virtues. He took ritual to mean the proper conventions in interactions between people, such as when a younger person greets an elder, or a state receives an official visit, or any formal human interaction. He believed that proper observation of these rituals was crucial to a functioning society.

Ritual propriety is understood as the proper relation to one's place in society, represented through traditional behaviours. Confucius strongly believed that a proper respect for ritual and one's role in society was an essential element of the superior person. It can be understood as a form of respect for others, and an act for the cohesion of society.

- **Trustworthiness**

Confucius believed that being reliable and trustworthy for other people was a key virtue. Again this is an example of how serving other people seems to be the guiding principle of his virtue ethics. This ties into the idea that ethics must serve the wider society and social cohesion as a whole:

> ***Make it your guiding principle to do your best for others and to be trustworthy in what you say, and move yourself to where rightness is, then you will be exalting virtue.***
> ***(Analects, 12:10)***

Trustworthiness is mentioned as a key virtue for young people to strive for so as to earn respect and be functioning members of society. Confucius understood that it was important in dealings between different social ranks, so as a ruler could take genuine advice or be trusted by his subjects when making difficult decisions.

- **Wisdom**

Confucius appealed against arrogance and falsehood, especially with regards to one's own knowledge. He believed that being honest with what you do not know was crucial to the proper functioning of society. That way educated people are able to make the proper decisions and those who need to learn are able and willing to.

The Master said, "Yu, shall I tell you what it is to know? To say you know when you know, and to say you do not when you do not, that is knowledge". (Analects, 2:7)

Evil

Confucius described evil (opposite to virtue) as a force which is inherent in the universe. It is something we can all indulge in and it is not to be understood as a particular property of one person. We cannot judge one person as 'evil', rather we can understand that their actions have partaken in evil. That way Confucius presented the (rather ahead of his time) principle of aiming to reform those who have done wrong, rather than to attack or judge them:

To attack evil as evil and not as evil of a particular man, is that not the way to reform the depraved? (Analects, 12:21)

This attitude speaks to a non-judgemental element of the Confucian world-view, which recognises the need for reform and justice in a society where all must live together.

Idle Talk & Gossip

Idle talk and gossip are traits which Confucius was disparaging of. We can assume that there are two main reasons for this. One that they can forment disunity, which works against the Confucian principle of social cohesion. The other that they distract one from their purpose, or work, which as mentioned is a virtue in itself.

The Master said, "The gossip-monger is the outcast of virtue". (Analects, 17:4)

Taken together these five virtues are guides to the behaviour which form Conufcius' ideal person. Confucius did not appeal to God, afterlife, soul or non material reason to justify his ethics. Instead, each virtue is carefully considered to form a peaceful and cohesive society. Each virtue is given with examples of how it can be enacted towards another person in a positive way, a clear indication that personal relations are at the heart of his philosophy. These virtues share non-selfishness, and consideration for others at their core.

Family

The family was regarded by Confucius as the primary social unit which forms the building blocks of the state. He encouraged men to work on their family, regulating their faults and errors, and keeping the unit in harmony. Confucius stressed traditional values of rearing one's children properly, and paying respect to elder family members.

Confucius designated the father as the head of the family, with lineage and rites being passed down via his side. Marriage was regarded as foundational to the family unit and a product of the proper relations between man and woman.

Regulating and educating one's own family was for Confucians a foundational building block to being a political ruler. Confucius did not consider anyone above this duty.

In order to govern the state, it is necessary first to regulate the family... it is not possible for one to teach others, while he cannot teach his own family...
(TGL, P.12)

In the works of Mencius, an idea of the 'five relationships' was formed, which later became synonymous with Confucian thought on family life and proper societal relationships. These are defined as those between father and son, between siblings, between husband and wife, between friends of different ages, and between ruler and subject.

Filial Piety

When parents are alive, they should be served according to propriety; when they are dead, they should be buried according to propriety; and they should be sacrificed according to propriety: —this may be called filial piety.
(Works of Meniscus, 3.2.1)

Filial piety is constantly referenced in the key texts. Filial piety means an attitude of respect (even devotion) to one's parents. A wish to obey them when younger, and care for them when they are older.

Filial piety has had an immense impact on Chinese culture, and to this day influences how the entire society functions.

Confucius regarded filial piety as foundational to benevolence and the other virtues, and an absolute cornerstone of a healthy nation. To disregard or dishonour one's parents, would have been the ultimate shame in Confucius' eyes.

Being respectful and obedient to one's parents at home is seen as the prerequisite to being a functioning member of society:

A young man should be a good son at home and an obedient young man abroad, sparing of speech but trustworthy in what he says...
(Analects, 1:6)

Sacrifices to ancestors are described with utmost importance and as a sign of respect to the past, the family unit and ultimately the entire community. These sacrifices form part of the less secular and more spiritual aspect of Confucian thought, although still serve a secular purpose as they contribute to the wider attitude of filial piety and ritual which bind society together.

> ***Conduct the funeral of your parents with meticulous care and let not sacrifices to your remote ancestors be forgotten, and the virtue of the common people will incline towards fullness.***
> ***(Analects, 1:9)***

Filial piety towards parents is regarded as a quality that should be extended outward In society, especially to those of valid authority such as a benevolent ruler.

Wealth

> ***If wealth were a permissible pursuit, I would be willing even to act as a guard holding a whip outside the marketplace. If it is not, I shall follow my own preferences.***
> ***(Analects, 7:12)***

Confucius famously lived a humble existence, never accumulating much wealth. He did not criticise the upper class of society who had it, however did stress the responsibility that came with power. He recognised the utility of wealth, but he did not regard wealth as a fundamental goal to strive for, preferring virtue, the arts, and personal cultivation over monetary gain.

He did stress the importance of acquiring wealth in a moral way if it is acquired and shunned those who stole or made money in a way which was not keeping with benevolence.

Wealth and high station are what men desire but unless I got them in the right way I would not remain in them.
(Analects, 4:5)

Politics

Much of Confucius' writing on politics and ruling seem to serve as a guidebook for a future ruler, who could use his teachings to govern a state harmoniously. This ruler would need to be a 'sage' as previously described, and of proper virtue and conduct.

Confucius believed that a ruler should earn his status through proper moral conduct rather than by lineage, such as in a traditional royal system. Ruler's were expected to set the example that their citizens should follow and their example would be so righteous that citizens would choose to follow out of respect, rather than coercion or control.

Confucius linked filial piety to the role of being a proper citizen or ruler and treated these qualities as interdependent. They are not the same thing though and he did give examples of where they can be in conflict. However it is clear that filial piety and proper family relations are core to Confucian politics.

Confucius placed emphasis on the proper behaviours and conduct of both the citizen and the ruler. He believed that each must properly enact their place in society for a cohesive state. He placed a high moral standard on rulers, who must be trustworthy, honest, pious and righteous so as to gain the moral authority to rule a state.

Let the ruler be a ruler, the subject a subject, the father a father, the son a son.
(Analects, 12:11)

The concept of democracy as we understand today did not exist in Confucius' era or culture. This would have probably run against his belief of society working within set roles. However this does not mean he envisaged a dictator who could rule with impunity. As with his other teachings, social cohesion formed the cornerstone from which his ideal ruler would operate. Therefore Confucius made if clear that a ruler must be trusted by his people:

...when there is no trust, the common people will have nothing to stand on
(Analects, 12:7)

Confucius also implied that governing should be by the consent of the people, who should want to be led by someone with the proper characteristics:

The Governor of She asked about government. The Master said, 'Ensure that those who are near are pleased and those who are far away are attracted.'
(Analects, 13:16)

Another example of his non-authoritarian style is that Confucius made it clear wealth should not be too centralised in the hands of the aristocratic class and should be well distributed across the state. This he believed was better for the common citizen, but also led to a more harmonious society and a longer lasting, more stable nation:

To centralise wealth is to disperse the people; to distribute wealth is to collect the people.
(The Great Learning, 5.9)

Education

If a ruler desires to transform the people, perfect customs, he can only do so through education!
(Xueji, I)

Confucius placed great emphasis on the importance of education, equally from the standpoint of a ruler educating his citizens, or a parent educating their child, or even a friend educating a friend. This is in keeping with the broader scope of Confucian philosophy to raise people up to act in a virtuous manner that benefits all.

Ritual and Ancestor Veneration

As mentioned, Confucius was intensely focused on ritual and the role it played in society. Ritual was often associated with the act of ancestor veneration. Worshipping and sacrificing to ancestors was not invented by Confucius, he himself saw it as a traditional activity that he needed to re-popularise for the moral betterment of society. His philosophy has now become synonymous with it.

Ritual was not limited to ancestor veneration, it also involved elaborate ceremonies when royal or political courts greeted others, or the proper arrangement of wedding and funeral events. Confucius believed that having proper structure and order to these ceremonies was a way of marking the important moments in society, and of course was key to maintaining social cohesion.

They served the dead as they would have served them when living; they served the departed as they would have served them, had they continued with them.
(The Doctorine of the Mean, 19.5)

Confucius, although largely secular in his writings, did seem to believe in a human soul or element of a person which was not bound by the death of the body. There is reference to the soul of a human surviving death, whilst an animal soul, and the human body do not.

That the bones and flesh should return to earth is what is appointed.
But the soul in its energy can go everywhere; it can go everywhere.
(Li Ki, bk.2, section 2, pt 3.13.)

The body and the animal soul go downwards; and the intelligent spirit is on high.
(Li Ki, bk.7, section 1.7)

He did not however seem to find a need to prove whether a soul had 'consciousness' after death, or to theorise in great detail as to the particular aspects of how a soul could exist outside of a body. It is taken as a given, or at least as a belief which serves society.

In this sense, ancestor veneration serves a few key purposes. One is to keep the family unit together, beyond the death of a parent, between generations. This serves to help the social cohesion of society as a whole, as family is the fundamental social unit.

As well as this, there is an implicit understanding that the 'soul' or immaterial aspect of a dead person is able to somehow perceive how their family behaves after their death. Therefore proper veneration of them, sacrifice to them, and continuation of their family work is treated with the utmost importance.

A family is understood to be able to accumulate the good or bad deeds of their parents and ancestors and in this vain the veneration and ritual of ancestor worship can serve to reinforce good deeds, or make penance for bad deeds which may disgrace a family.

The fact that sacrifice and belief in spirits is so closely related to family is evident. Confucius warned against offering sacrifice to those out of your own family, viewing it as unnecessary.

To offer sacrifice to the spirit of an ancestor not one's own is obsequious.
(Analects, 2:24)

Sacrifice to ancestors took the form of a ceremony, the detail and expense of which depended on the social class of the family. The eldest son was expected to preside over the ceremony as the new head of the family. Sacrifices of food and drink were often made to ancestors and even occasionally live animals, although there is little mention of this practice.

Sacrifice to ancestors was not a common event for most families during Confucius' era and usually took place on the anniversary of a death and perhaps at other important events in the year such as the advent of spring or autumn.

Confucius regarded the act of ancestor veneration as a necessary ritual that should be done sincerely, as he believed if it was done casually it would be useless. He did however make it clear that contact with or study of the metaphysical or spiritual realms was not to be a primary duty, or to be concentrated on above daily life. It was instead something to be done rarely, with respect.

To work for the things the common people have a fight to and to keep one's distance from the gods and spirits while showing them reverence can be called wisdom.
(Analects, 6:22)

This is consistent with the clear thread in Confucian thought, that above all, service to the society and social structure was the primary Good.

Confucius often references 'Tian', a Chinese word translated roughly as 'heaven' or 'sky' and is a reference to the traditional Chinese view of astrology or fate. He does not use this as a justification for his teachings, or ever claim men do not have free will due to fate, but he does nod to the utility of 'heaven' playing a role in the affairs of humans and refers to it as the cause of his virtue.

Heaven is author of the virtue that is in me...
(Analects, 7:23)

The Arts

Practice of the Arts is another important aspect of Confucianism. He strongly believed that arts are an essential element of society which enrich the human experience. Practising the traditional arts was seen as a vital component of being a 'Sage' or 'Gentleman', and not just an optional leisure pursuit. Recreation in artistic form, whether that meant producing or consuming art, was seen as beneficial to the person and to society as a whole.

Confucian texts refer to a range of art forms, particularly poetry (odes) and music. Confucius was well versed in traditional 'odes' and believed they carried moral virtue and teachings at their essence:

> ***The Odes are three hundred in number. They can be summed up in one phrase, not Swerving from the right path.***
> ***(Analects, 2:2)***

He encouraged his disciples to study the odes, and reminded them of their importance, not just as an art, but also in their application to life:

> ***Why is it none of you, my young friends, study the Odes? An apt quotation from the Odes may serve to stimulate the imagination, to show one's breeding, to smooth over difficulties in a group and to give expression to complaints.***
> ***(Analects, 17:9)***

Clearly, Confucius was taken by music. He is thought to have been a singer himself and also a critic of music. Evidence of this is in *the Analects* where it is said he would join in on others' songs. He loved hearing others play or sing, and found joy in the pleasure of music.

Music produces pleasure which human nature cannot be without. (Li Ki, bk.17, section 3)

Confucius is thought to have authored or dictated a text *'The Book of Music',* which was unfortunately lost and is unable to now be restored. Music was an important part of the 'rites' and rituals that a royal or political court would engage in to celebrate events of welcome guests.

Ceremonies and music should not for a moment be neglected by anyone. (Li Ki, bk.17, section 3.23)

The Master was singing in the company of others and liked someone else's song, he always asked to -hear it again before joining in. (Analects, 7:32)

Confucius also referred to a spiritual or metaphysical aspect to music. He did not only regard it as a leisure, or ritualistic pursuit. Rather, he recognised that music can reflect the beauty and order of nature and the universe, and was a way of accessing a greater understanding of life:

In music of the grandest style there is the same harmony that prevails between Heaven and Earth; in ceremonies of the grandest form there is the same graduation that exists between Heaven and Earth. (Li Ki, bk.17, section 1.19)

Confucian philosophy is above all a guide to living a virtuous life, with personal conduct, family, ritual, and the arts given as the foundations to achieving the objective of an ethical and stable community. The impact of Confucian philosophy on Eastern Asia, and later the Western world is hard to measure. Perhaps no other philosophy has influenced so many people over time.

Confucianism, like any other philosophy, is not an 'island', and is part of the societal context it grew in, absorbing many already existing ancient Chinese concepts. In fact in many ways it is an attempt to salvage pre existing traditions and rights. It is a humanistic philosophy, which appeals to principles which are not derived from religion, or the concept of salvation or an afterlife.

There is of course reference to what may be considered supernatural in the form of ritual rights and venerating the dead and mention of concepts such as soul and death. However these are certainly not the justification or the cornerstone of Confucius' works.

When asked how he strives to live, Confucius encapsulated his teachings in one sentence:

I set my heart on the Way, base myself on virtue, lean upon benevolence for support and take my recreation in the arts.
(Analects, 7:6)

SOURCES:

Entire Book:

Chan, W. (1969). *A source book in Chinese philosophy.* Princeton, NJ: Princeton University Press.

Radhakrishnan, S., & Moore, C. A. (1957). *A sourcebook in Indian philosophy.* Princeton, NJ: Princeton University Press.

Yoga Chapter:

Bharati, S. V. (2001). *Yoga Sutras of Patanjali* (Vol. 3). Motilal Banarsidass Publ.

Iyenger, B. K. (2006). *Light on yoga.* New Delhi: Harpercollins.

Madhusudhan Saraswati, (1998) Gambhiranada Swami. *Bhagavad Gita.* Himalaya: Advaita Ashrama.

Mass, Phillip, (2013) *A Concise Historiography of Classical Yoga Philosophy, p. 53-90.*

Mukerji, P. N., H. Ā., P., Hariharananda, S. A. (1983). *Yoga Philosophy of Patanjali: Containing His Yoga Aphorisms with Vyasa's*

Commentary in Sanskrit and a Translation with Annotations Including Many Suggestions for the Practice of Yoga. United States: State University of New York Press.

Patañjali, Jha, G., Sastri, S. S., Vyāsa, & Vācaspatimiśra. (2002). *The Yoga-darshana: Comprising the sūtras of Patañjali, with the bhāstya of Vyāsa.* Fremont, California, Asian Humanities Press.

Patañjali, Mukerji, P. N., & Āranya, H. (1983). *Yoga philosophy of Patañjali: Containing his Yoga aphorisms with commentary of Vyāsa's commentary in sanskrit and a translation with annotations including many suggestions for the practice of Yoga.* Albany, NY: State University of New York Press.

Śarmā, C. (1962). *Indian Philosophy a critical survey.* New York: Barnes & Noble.

Schweizer, P. (1993). *Mind/Consciousness Dualism in Sankhya-Yoga Philosophy. Philosophy and Phenomenological Research, 53*(4), 845. doi:10.2307/2108256.

Nyaya Chapter:

Chakrabarti, K. (1975). T*he Nyāya-Vaisheshika theory of universals. Journal of Indian Philosophy, 3*(3-4), 363-382. doi:10.1007/bf02629152

Chakrabarti, K. K. (2010). *Classical Indian philosophy of induction: the Nyaya viewpoint.* Lexington Books. ISSN: 2320-2882.

Guha, D. C. (1979). *Navya Nyāya System of Logic: Basic Theories & Techniques.*

Gotama, Vidyabhusana, S. C., & Basu, B. D. (1974). *The sacred books of the Hindus.* New York: AMS Pr.

Lakra, Rajen. (2018). *Universals in Nyaya-vaisesika school*, International Journal of Creative Research Thoughts Volume 6.

Matilal, B.K., 1986. *Perception: An Essay on Classical Indian Theories of Knowledge*, Oxford: Oxford University Press.

Phillips, Stephen, "Epistemology in Classical Indian Philosophy", *The Stanford Encyclopedia of Philosophy* (Spring 2019 Edition), Edward N. Zalta (ed.), URL = <https://plato.stanford.edu/archives/spr2019/entries/epistemology-india/>.

Buddhism Chapter:

Anuradha Sutta: To Anuradha (SN 22.86), translated from the Pali by Thanissaro Bhikkhu. *Access to Insight (BCBS Edition)*, 30 November 2013, http://www.accesstoinsight.org/tipitaka/sn/sn22/sn22.086.than.html .

Anonymous, (2013) *"Theravada Buddhism: A Chronology"*. Access to Insight (BCBS Edition), URL= http://www.accesstoinsight.org/history.html.

Byrom, T. (2010). *The Dhammapada: The sayings of the Buddha.* London: Ebury Digital.

Bodhi, B. (2012). *The Numerical Discourses of the Buddha A Complete Translation of the Anguttara Nikaya*. New York: Wisdom Publications.

Buddhaghosa, Warren, H. C., & Kosambi, D. D. (1989). *The Visuddhimagga of Buddhaghosâcariya*. Delhi: Motilal Banarsidass Publ.

Harvey, P. (2013). *An introduction to Buddhism teachings, history and practises.* Cambridge: Cambridge Univ. Press.

Itivuttaka: The Group of Ones (Iti 1-27), translated from the Pali by Thanissaro Bhikkhu. *Access to Insight (BCBS Edition)*, 30 November 2013, http://www.accesstoinsight.org/tipitaka/kn/iti/iti.1.001-027.than.html .

Maha-satipatthana Sutta: The Great Frames of Reference" (DN 22), translated from the Pali by Thanissaro Bhikkhu. *Access to Insight (BCBS Edition)*, 30 November 2013, http://www.accesstoinsight.org/tipitaka/dn/dn.22.0.than.html.

Maurice, D. (1967). *The lion's roar; an anthology of the Buddha's teachings selected from the Pali canon*. New York: Citadel Press.

Paccaya Sutta: Requisite Conditions" (SN 12.20), translated from the Pali by Thanissaro Bhikkhu. *Access to Insight (BCBS Edition)*, 30 November 2013, http://www.accesstoinsight.org/tipitaka/sn/sn12/sn12.020.than.html .

Robinson, R. H., Johnson, W. L., Thānissaro, & Robinson, R. H. (2005). *Buddhist religions: A historical introduction*. Belmont, CA: Wadsworth/Thomson.

Siderits, Mark, "Buddha", *The Stanford Encyclopedia of Philosophy* (Spring 2019 Edition), Edward N. Zalta (ed.), URL = <https://plato.stanford.edu/archives/spr2019/entries/buddha/>.

Thanissaro Bhikkhu. (1999) *"The Four Noble Truths: A Study Guide"* Access to Insight (BCBS Edition), 30 November 2013. URL= http://www.accesstoinsight.org/lib/study/truths.html .

Taoism Chapter:

Cua, A. S. (1981). *Opposites as Complements: Reflections on the Significance of Tao. Philosophy East and West, 31*(2), 123. doi:10.2307/1399136.

Hansen, Chad, "Daoism", *The Stanford Encyclopedia of Philosophy* (Spring 2020 Edition), Edward N. Zalta (ed.), URL = <https://plato.stanford.edu/archives/spr2020/entries/daoism/>.

Kohn, L. (2004). *Cosmos and community: The ethical dimension of Daoism.* Three Pines Press.

Laozi, & Mitchell, S. (2006). *Tao te ching: A new English version.* New York: HarperCollins.

Zhuangzi, & Merton, T. (1969). *The way of Chuang Tzu by Thomas Merton. (Third printing.).* New York: New Directions.

Confucianism Chapter:

Confucius, & Dawson, M. M. (1915). *The ethics of Confucius the sayings of the master and his disciples upon the conduct of "the superior man".* New York: Putnam.

Confucius, & Lau, D. C. (2000). *The Analects.* Columbia: Columbia University Press.

Csikszentmihalyi, Mark, "Confucius", *The Stanford Encyclopedia of Philosophy* (Summer 2020 Edition), Edward N. Zalta (ed.), URL <https://plato.stanford.edu/archives/sum2020/entries/confucius/>.

Di, X., & MacEwan, H. (2017). *Chinese philosophy on teaching and learning: Xueji in the twenty-first century.* Albany, NY: State University of New York Press.

Hall, D. L., & Ames, R. T. (1987). *Thinking through confucius. Suny Press.*

Legge, J. (1894). *The four books: Confucian analects, the great learning, the doctrine of mean and the Works of Mencius.* Shanghai: Chinese Book.

Yu, J. (2013). *The ethics of Confucius and Aristotle: Mirrors of virtue* (Vol. 7). Routledge.

Printed in Great Britain
by Amazon

12010571R10086